Dedication

To Colleen whose love and support inspires me daily and to Rich, Paul, Chris and Laurel who are my constant reminder why we make leadership a way of life for their future!

Printed in the United States of America
First Printing 2014

ISBN-13: 978-0615903545
RPC Books
www.imjustsayinbook.com

A Branded Imprint of

RPC Books
rpcleadershipassociates.com

Acknowlegments

Successful business books, like successful leaders, do not happen by chance. This one evolved over five years to become the version you are reading now. It is solely based on the feedback and insights from clients, prospects, readers, students and supporters of the RPC Leadership Associates, Inc. Vision to make Leadership a Way of Life. This is their book!

Many thanks to those who provided their candid insights into the best articles and stories that should go into this book. Sadly, one of the most consistent readers passed away this year quite unexpectedly. Peter Sturdivant was not only a good friend; he was an active thought-partner when it came to leadership as a way of life. I will miss his challenging discussions and ideas, and most important, his friendship.

I once again called on a very talented group of professionals to help make this second book a reality. As with the first book, each took on a piece of the project as if it were their own. The editing by Danielle Willis proved invaluable to create a great finished product. The cover graphics from Paul Feith at Paul Gregory Media helped set the tone for the stories told between the covers. His collaboration with Jeff Ross of Jeff Ross Studios created the winning formula for the cover graphics. Julia Newton at Archer Media Services created the layout to optimize the overall experience for the reader. And once again, Sarah Bruns of InGauge, Inc. created an online presence that artfully captures the spirit of the book. It feels great knowing we have this team supporting our publishing efforts. They make it look and feel easier than I am sure it is!

And finally, I cannot thank my family enough for their ongoing unconditional support, patience and insights. Everyone helped in some way to bring it all together and you continue to inspire me.

Thank You!

Table of Contents

Table of Contents (continued)

Table of Contents (continued)

Introduction

When RPC Leadership Associates, Inc. was created in July 2008, we set out to update the way leadership and leadership development was thought of and executed across the small and mid-sized for-profit and non-profit landscape. A key element of our Vision and Strategy was to approach leadership development from an attitudinal perspective. We believe leaders have to think like leaders before they can become leaders, regardless of what it says on their business card! While this concept sounds simple and straightforward, it is anything but in practice.

In the years since we started, several key messages evolved through our work with corporate leadership teams, individual professionals, entrepreneurs and business owners as well as non-profit leaders. Phrases like "Hope is Not a Strategy," "What you Believe you Think and what you Think you Do" and "Well Done is better than Well Said" have come to represent our work and the sustainable success our clients achieved by first "thinking" like leaders and then naturally becoming better leaders.

In those same years, we wrote monthly articles about what it takes to think like a leader and addressed topics that were top-of-mind for our clients, prospects and readers. Based on their feedback, we took the best ideas from the past, combining them with new never before published ideas and created *I'm Just Sayin'… Revelations for Making Leadership a Way of Life.*

No matter where you open this book there is an idea related to the attitudinal aspect of leadership. Within these 52 quick-read ideas lay the foundation for your own journey to making Leadership a Way of Life. Read them once a week or read many at one time. But don't just read them! Read them and apply them in the context of your own leadership situation!

Enjoy the Book!

Section I:
Personal Leadership

"Become the kind of leader that people would follow voluntarily; even if you had no title or position."

~ Brian Tracy

Leadership starts with leading ourselves. If we cannot effectively lead ourselves, we have little right to ask others to follow us anywhere. This section is about the things we need to embrace to effectively think like and, ultimately, behave like lifelong leaders!

Section 1: Personal Leadership

Everyone looks like an effective leader...
until the enemy shows up

This was an oft-repeated message to my leaders when I was in the military. For those who have been in the military can relate to the notion of endless days and weeks training to be at the top of your craft when we were ever needed to enter the field of battle. The events since September 2001 and their impact on the military created a renewed sense of urgency and the preparation needed to always be ready to lead.

Early in my tenure as a new manager at my first company after the military, we were hit with a catastrophic event that crippled most of our telecommunications network on the east coast. While Mother Nature was the cause, it was up to us to take the right actions to help our customers (business clients) work around the issue. Though it was early in my management tenure, I had already formed an impression of the capabilities of my team members. After the crisis was over, I once again had to assess my team's individual capabilities. Much to my chagrin, the before and after lists were very different. The enemy (Mother Nature) had shown up unexpectedly and not all the team was able to step up as we might have thought them capable.

I once had the privilege of meeting LTG(R) Hal Moore and Mr. Joe Galloway. You may remember them portrayed by Mel Gibson and Barry Pepper respectively in the movie We Were Soldiers Once...And Young. When asked what leadership lesson he took away from his experiences, General Moore simply, and without hesitation, stated "Lead by Example". Real leadership, you see, is leading from the front of the organization where you face the enemy, turn to your organization and, with confidence, say – Follow Me.

Today, the enemy is staggering uncertainty driven by a sluggish economic recovery, political positioning and in-fighting and global unrest. Now is the time to take stock of your personal leadership brand and your organization's leadership culture and see if anyone is following.

Who is following you in the face of the enemy?

Lead Well!

Section I: Personal Leadership

Leadership is a Habit –
Do You Believe It and Are You Practicing It?

Everyone has leadership potential, but not everyone uses that potential to its fullest measure. More often than not, it is because leadership, and I mean great leadership, takes us on a journey requiring repetitive practice and an unwavering attitude towards changing our performance. But is it possible to create new leadership habits?

Research tells us that once old habits are burned into the part of the brain responsible for short-term memory (the hippocampus, if you will), they are there to stay. We also know that just over 75% of these habits are negatively influenced as we grew up (Why is "No" generally one of the first words we learn?). New habits come from getting out of our comfort zone and reaching into our stretch zone – where true change occurs. If we focus on incremental and continuous change, what the Japanese call "Kaizen," we can then manage the normal fear that comes with change. If the change becomes too great too fast, fear escalates to the point we enter the stress zone which may invoke a flight or fight response.

In a 2008 New York Times article entitled "Can you Become Creatures of New Habits?", Ms. M. J. Ryan, author of This Year I Will…, states, "I apprentice myself to someone when I want to learn something new or develop a new habit."

New attitudes create new habits of thought, replacing old habits to create effective sustained leadership. Apprenticing under someone else or being coached helps ensure the new habits are the right habits.

Who are you apprenticing under to create new success habits?

Lead Well!

Section I: Personal Leadership

*"Now is the Time for Action…
Not Fear! "*

We are all familiar with Franklin D. Roosevelt's words:

"…the only thing we have to fear is fear itself - nameless, unreasoning, unjustified terror which paralyzes needed efforts to convert retreat into advance."

He said these words at the beginning of his inaugural speech on March 4, 1933. As I read through the entire inaugural address to understand his full context, it occurred to me he was speaking about Leadership, both his and that of the citizenry of that time. Fast-forward to today and we find the message of leadership remains resolute. A tough economic environment is not really the headline. The real headline is whether we allow ourselves to get caught up in the fear associated with tough times.

While I, like many others, was negatively impacted by the last recession, the weaker economy, poor consumer confidence and uncertain stock markets do not affect my focus on my personal and professional Goals and Vision. A recession had no sway over our desire and ability to help organizations, individual professionals and students achieve sustained success when times are good as well as when times are tough. FDR's words were a call to action for improved results, a call to action not unlike what I am suggesting now.

As we take stock of our circumstances and craft our plan of action to advance, I believe we have two choices. We can wait for someone to tell us what to do next, a bailout of sorts. Or we can reach out to someone (mentor, adviser, coach etc.) who can help hold us accountable for taking the actions necessary to achieve improved results and sustained success.

Who will you reach out to for support?

Lead Well!

Section I: Personal Leadership

"Leadership…
is Salesmanship"

I first came across this quote when I read Hamid "Hank" Noorani's book, *"POWER – The Modern Doctrine"* and had a chance to explore the idea in a video interview we did together several years ago. It caught my attention because those who know me as a Leadership and Business Coach are surprised that I am also a Sales Coach. I have always believed there is a level of genuine salesmanship in the process of being an effective leader. While I would be the first to agree the two are not identical twins, I would also argue they are at least in the same family tree!

One of the key arguments they are not alike, I believe, stems from an outdated understanding of 21st Century Salesmanship. For instance, in Daniel Pink's latest book To Sell is Human, he makes multiple cases for the human element of sales as opposed to the fast-talking, hard pressing salesman profiled in so many books and movies like Glengarry Glen Ross and The Boiler Room. At the very end of the book, he asks the reader if, after persuading someone to buy something, to ask and answer two questions

1. "If the person you're selling to agrees to buy, will his or her life improve?"
2. "When your interaction is over, will the world be a better place than when you began?"

"If the answer to either of these questions is "No", you're doing something wrong." It seems clear that these same questions can be applied to the leader's interaction with their followers.

Dwight D. Eisenhower once said, "Leadership is the art of getting someone else to do something you want done because he/she wants to do it." What he is referring to is the power of persuasion. Persuasion is an adjective often, and easily, associated with both Salesmanship and Leadership. But when we think of persuasion in the 21st Century, we look at it from a very collaborative and relational viewpoint. The hard-selling tactics or authoritarian leadership tactics of the past carry little sway in today's business environment.

As you lead your business, what are your followers buying from you?

Lead (Sell) Well!

Section 1: Personal Leadership

*"The illiterate of the 21st Century will not be those who
cannot read or write...
but those who cannot learn, unlearn and relearn"*

This quote from Alvin Toffler, noted author and futurist is a great
way to put us in the mindset of this topic: Dealing with Change.
The ability to "learn, unlearn and relearn" is, in my mind, one of the
crucial, core attributes of successful leadership in today's dynamic
business environment.

Consider the results of a 2009 survey by McKinsey & Company of
more than 1,600 executives, senior managers and mid-level managers
worldwide who were asked about how well they had responded to the
then-current economic crisis. Respondents were asked to rate their
level of satisfaction as a business leader in various areas. What caught
my eye were three categories that are particularly telling in the area of
leading change in today's environment. They are (percentages are %
very satisfied with performance):

	C-Suite	Mid-Mgmt
Retaining, attracting talented people	35%	26%
Positioning company for growth	34%	27%
Developing people's leadership capabilities so they can manage crisis	29%	25%

Why did only a third of C-level executives and roughly a quarter of mid-
level managers feel they are doing very well in adapting to change?
From my own 30 years of experience, I offer three reasons why this
might be the case.

Section 1: Personal Leadership

Wait it out – Embracing a "wait it out" strategy by definition puts the organization behind their competitors. Forward thinking leaders continue to use the recession as a means to re-evaluate their strategies and re-tool their businesses for the new realities of the business, political and service economy. A wait-and-see leader will only be able to react to the new environment with little leverage to dictate direction like their forward thinking counterparts.

Unprepared culture – I suspect the organizations that were not very satisfied with their performance in these areas were not doing very well in the same areas before the crisis. Their culture was not likely built on a platform of continuous change. By instilling an evolutionary mindset to change in the hearts and minds of the organization, a leader will be in a much better position to make the crucial decisions necessary to embrace a crisis head-on.

Lack of people skills – Change is an emotional process. Leaders who are not comfortable leading in a culture of accountability, transparency and empathy are doomed to lag behind because of their limitations with these crucial people skills. Change cannot be successful without people embracing it as positive, a mindset the leader must enable through open and transparent communications.

How are you handling the new realities?

Lead Well!

Section I: Personal Leadership

"Leadership Lessons...
from Running Triathlons"

Every year since 2007, I have run a Sprint Triathlon in our hometown. In 2010, I had the privilege of running it with my youngest son who was running the race for the first time. Since it was his first race and our plan was to run it together, our motto for the race became "Start Steady, Finish Strong." The Sprint Triathlon is the shortest of the four official distances but still involves the same three events – swimming, biking and running, in that order. As I reflected back on the race, it occurred to me the parallels between training and running triathlons with leadership coaching.

When I first began competing in triathlons, I viewed each leg as separate events in which to train. I was a competitive swimmer and runner in both high school and college so it was natural for me to train in each event as I had before. This is no different when we find ourselves approaching new professional and personal challenges by relying on the skills and knowledge we developed from our past. Even when we set goals for ourselves to improve in an individual endeavor, the past will govern our execution unless we consciously make a change. And as I realized my training regimen wasn't enough, I needed to make a change – in my attitude regarding the race itself!

I actually made two changes to my mental approach to the race to ultimately achieve my goal. First, I changed my mental approach to the race from three individual events back-to-back-to-back to one race with five aligned competitive pieces. I say five because the transitions between events are really mini-events in and by themselves as the clock continues to tick during the swim-bike and bike-run transitions. Secondly, I realized I could not do this solely based on my own experience. I reached out to accomplished tri-athletes and sought advice from others who were also trying to optimize their triathlon experience.

Section I: Personal Leadership

What does this have to do with leadership? How much are you relying on old habits of the past to deal with today's challenges? Are you going about change alone or are you reaching out to others to help you develop new leadership attitudes? Is your business a series of disparate, misaligned goals preventing you from achieving your ultimate objective? These are questions all leaders should regularly ask themselves.

Fred Lebow, founder of the New York City Marathon, a race I've run twice, once said, "In running, it doesn't matter whether you come in first, in the middle of the pack or last. You can say 'I finished'. There is a lot of satisfaction in that." As my son and I completed the triathlon, I had no idea where in the pack we finished, but I do know we Started Steady and we definitely Finished Strong!

How are your goals aligned for a strong finish?

Lead Well!

Section 1: Personal Leadership

"Being 'Above Average' is to Success...
what being 'Above Ground' is to Living"

This quote is from Jay Niblick's book *What's your Genius*. It struck a chord with me when I first read it, and as I sat down to pen this article on achieving success, it resonated once again. I believe it speaks to success being more than just getting by, much like truly living life is determined by more than simply standing upright and breathing.

I find it interesting how rarely I hear the term "Success" before it happens. At the end of fiscal cycle, I typically hear many variations of "We succeeded because..." or "Look what we did to succeed." What I hear little of at the beginning of a fiscal cycle are phrases like "Here's what we will do to succeed" or "Our success looks like..." It is as if we only feel comfortable talking about success after it happens. We seem less comfortable planning for success and overtly stating how we will achieve it. Too often we throw together a loosely defined plan and hope it works.

Having goals helps you identify what you want to do and why you want to achieve them. However, you also have to be capable of achieving success. Do you possess the skills (the know how) required to be successful? Additionally, do you have the knowledge (the know when and know where) to use your skills in their proper context?

We spend a good deal of time, many times the majority of our time, developing our skills and knowledge, believing they will help us achieve our goals and ultimately be successful. But is it enough?

Not really! One only has to listen to the battlefield of broken resolutions that typically show themselves the beginning of every New Year.

Section I: Personal Leadership

With great intentions, so many set goals to improve themselves aptly equipped with the skills and knowledge to do so. Yet by the end of the first three months, they begin to break down. What's missing? Attitude makes the difference. It defines our want to achieve our goal and be the success we have pictured in our mind's eye. While attitude contributes to nearly 75% of our success, how much time do we spend developing our attitude? Probably significantly less than 75%! Instead, we continue to invest heavily in skills and knowledge hoping they will make up the difference. They won't!

The right combination of Goals, Skills, Knowledge and Attitudes provides us our greatest opportunity to create a future of success. In a Victor Hugo quote forwarded to me recently, he states, "The future has many names. For the weak, it means unattainable. For the fearful, it means the unknown. For the courageous, it means opportunity."

How will you muster the courage to live more than "above ground"?

Lead Well!

Section I: Personal Leadership

*"Discipline is the refining fire…
by which talent becomes ability"*

No matter how much leadership development, management training or personal coaching we attend or participate in, successful leadership must always include a discussion of discipline. This reference by Roy L. Smith is a great example of the crucial role discipline plays in our success as leaders. In one of my earliest newsletters, I spoke of talent and what it really takes to create the ability to be a successful leader. In the years since, I have had the pleasure of working with successful entrepreneurs, organizational leadership teams and not-for-profit leaders and boards. In every case, the ability to be disciplined leaders contributes to their sustainable success.

I recently had the privilege of attending a seminar by a fellow coach who spoke of the value of 10,000 hours. If you have read Malcolm Gladwell's book *Outliers,* you know about the 10,000 hours. He speaks to the idea that it takes 10,000 hours of purposeful practice to become an expert in your field. If we are to be expert leaders, we need to have practiced successful leadership for at least that many hours. In simpler terms, 10,000 hours breaks down to nearly 3 hours per day for 10 years! It means that for at least 3 hours a day, you have the discipline to be the leader you need to be so that it becomes second nature to you.

Therein lies the issue with leadership development as we used to know it. You cannot go to a class or attend a seminar and walk out a leader no more than you can take a few golf lessons and play like a pro. When professional golfers practice their golf swing at the practice range, each shot is taken with a purpose in mind. Each shot has significance and contributes to their ability to win the next tournament making the practice time meaningful to success on the course.

Section 1: Personal Leadership

So too, leadership is also about leading with a purpose. I recently gave a presentation titled "Keeping Your Business in Alignment with Your Purpose." In order to do this, you must know what your purpose is. It is entirely possible we became organizational leaders without a specific purpose in mind. Possibly our purpose is still unfolding as we continue to exercise our leadership abilities. And possibly our purpose has changed as we evolve as leaders through our 10,000 hour leadership journey.

Whatever the case, having the discipline to make each hour, each day, each week as a leader count towards becoming the expert leader your followers are looking to you for must become your purpose.

How are you keeping the refining fire lit?

Lead Well!

Section 1: Personal Leadership

"Well Done…
Is better than Well Said"

When we speak of Authenticity, we discern who we really are behind the behavior that represents what the outside world sees of us. Leaders especially are faced with crucial decisions that may challenge their ability to be authentic. What they have to fall back on in tough situations is their integrity. It is a value often thrown around like a buzzword, and we, unfortunately, see the results of a lack of integrity around us in business, politics and even sports.

In his 1996 book *"Integrity"*, Yale Law Professor Stephen L. Carter writes that integrity requires three steps: "*discerning* what is right and what is wrong; *acting* on what you have discerned, even at personal cost; and *saying openly* that you are acting on your understanding of right from wrong." Each of these points is crucial to being a true leader of integrity.

Discerning what is right and wrong is a function of our personal values. We know what our true personal values are because they never waver regardless of the situation. They show up consistently when everyone is watching as much as when nobody is looking. They are also appreciated above and beyond our talents such that the two (values and talents) are never confused with each other nor are they ever viewed out of order in priority.

Saying what we believe also reflects our authentic self, only now we become visible and public. Of course, it is also now easy to create or manufacture a script we want others to hear, whether or not it is in alignment with our true beliefs and core values. In this environment especially, it is often risky for leaders to say what they truly believe.

Lastly, it boils down to what people see their leaders do. Leadership behavior becomes the ultimate barometer of integrity in that followers see the congruence between what their leaders say and what their leaders do.

Section I: Personal Leadership

The best example of this in my mind takes me back to the Honor Code as a West Point Cadet. It states, "A cadet will not lie, cheat or steal or tolerate those who do." The first part of the code is easier to do than the second part because inaction (tolerating those who do) is just as detrimental as poor action. Followers ultimately pass their final judgment on their leaders based on this behavior.

What we believe, we think. What we think, we do. What we do generates desired results. This is the essence of leadership and is at the core of being a leader with integrity when our beliefs, attitudes and actions all tell the same story.

How many of your followers will say to you - "Well done"?

Lead Well!

Section 1: Personal Leadership

*"In the long run, we get no more...
than we are willing to risk giving"*

One of the components of success is reflecting on how successful a previous business cycle has been (in this case, a year). I always go back to my Vision and validate how I lived the Vision throughout the past year. I review how we helped "Make Leadership a Way of Life" for our clients. It occurred to me, in every case, some level of risk was involved. Whether it is the risk of change, the risk of being wrong or the risk of being right, risk is an essential part of effective leadership.

The journey to successful lifelong leadership begins, like any other journey, with a sense of where you are right now. The trick is to realistically assess your performance, your strengths and weaknesses and your current capabilities as well as those of your competitors. Realistic is not necessarily conservative or leading edge. It can be those extremes or anything in between. The key is that it be based on real knowledge of the markets, industries and organizational capabilities such that the strategy truly minimizes risk and optimizes success.

Successful lifelong leadership is developed through continuous and measurable performance. While activities are the stepping-stones of achieving desired results, lifelong leaders know they are merely the means to the end. Leaders who can paint a vivid picture of what the desired performance looks like in the next several business cycles have a much greater chance of success for their organizations and themselves. Ask yourself – "What will I be doing, saying, writing about this time next year? What are my clients saying about me and what are they posting on social media sites about our business?"

Lastly, being a successful lifelong leader involves change. Embracing change is inherently risky, yet it is what every lifelong leader MUST do as a matter of course. In a global economy where technology and cultural influences keep the landscape in a constant state of flux, being a leader is risky. As the late great UCLA basketball coach John Wooden said, "Failure is not fatal, but failure to change might be.

The question becomes less of "Is this decision risky?" and more so "How risky is this decision?" Being a successful lifelong leader entails making crucial decisions without the benefit of all the necessary information. It means being comfortable with the possibility that a very risky decision may be the best decision under the circumstances.

The answer to mitigating risk in each of the three scenarios above begins with a Vision to help frame what being Realistic means, what level of Performance is required and how much Change is necessary to realize the Vision.

As you review your Vision, how much are you willing to risk giving?

Lead Well!

Section 1: Personal Leadership

*"Wisdom is the Power…
to put our Time and our Knowledge to the Proper Use"*

Time Management is one of the more important and popular leadership topics I am asked to speak about in my workshops. Knowledge, as a function of effective decision-making and communications, is integrated into nearly every workshop I facilitate. It occurs to me addressing both in the context of this quote by Thomas J. Watson, former Chairman and CEO of IBM, made sense in today's time and knowledge strained business environment.

We've all heard the expression "Time is Money." We know money is either spent or invested. When we invest money, we expect a return on our investment. When we spend money, we consume what we buy as a one-time event. Time is no different in the sense that it, like money, is either spent or invested. When we spend time, we never get it back as it is a one-time event. When we invest time, we have an expectation of some level of return for the time invested. The difference between spending time and investing time is the presence of goals. When time is used towards accomplishing our goals, we are making an investment in our personal and professional future. When we do not have goals, time used is spent on one-and-done events, which do little to advance our future.

We live in a world that is information-rich and knowledge-poor. We can get content from anywhere through the wonders of modern technology and the plethora of data sources available to us in real time. However, it takes a level of understanding and time to put the content into a context resulting in sustainable leadership decisions. It is knowledge which helps leaders know when and where to effectively leverage their leadership skills. When leaders rely only on information, as far too many do in my experience, their decisions have limited effectiveness for their organization. True knowledge-based decisions and communications provide deeper meaning and understanding for all in the organization.

Section I: Personal Leadership

The implication to today's leader is clear. They are increasingly challenged with where they invest time and deal with volumes more information to convert to knowledge than existed in the days of Thomas J. Watson. The key element to tackling both is having clear, written goals that align to the leader's purpose and vision in a very specific, measureable and time-bound manner. In this way, time is invested towards goal achievement and only relevant information becomes knowledge to achieve desired results.

It is wisdom that forms the foundation of sustainable leadership. Wisdom based on the effective investment of time and the efficient use of knowledge to become life-long leaders.

How are your goals taking you down the road to Wisdom?

Lead Well!

Section I: Personal Leadership

"I am a Runner!"

As I discussed before, I am a triathlete. I started running a local sprint triathlon in 2007 with the expressed goal of completing the quarter-mile swim, the thirteen-mile bike and the five-kilometer run in under an hour and a half. For six years I entered with the same goal and for six years I came close without achieving my desired result. Each year I analyzed the results of each event to see how to train smarter, recognizing that with each passing year I also got older. I kept getting close to my goal but never reached it…

…until I changed my affirmation attached to my goal. My previous affirmation centered on being in good physical shape and having a positive mental attitude towards the race itself. However, it was not helping me mentally where I needed it the most, finishing the run without walking. So I changed my affirmation to "I am a Runner" and said it aloud during all my training runs and during the race. The result: One hour, twenty-six minutes, fifty-six seconds! Goal achieved!

So what exactly is an affirmation? An affirmation is: "telling yourself in times of doubt that which you know to be true at other times." More specifically, it is a positive statement which describes the "you" you want to become through your goals.

Through the conscious and effective use of affirmations we are able to program our subconscious mind so that it operates as a success mechanism and causes positive behavior and change towards the achievement of our goals.

Section I: Personal Leadership

The power of affirmations is best recognized when we realize that the mind doesn't know the difference between real and imagined. For example, suppose you "imagine" late at night that there is a burglar in your house. Are you any less frightened than if you "knew" there was a burglar in your house? Of course not! You are afraid because you imagine a fearful situation. The use of affirmations to build confidence applies to the same principle, but with a positive goal in mind.

Our success is tied to our actions and our actions to our attitude. Thus, the "automatic guidance system" within us either operates as a success mechanism or failure mechanism. It all depends on the goals we set for it.

What will motivate you to achieve your most challenging goals?

Lead Well!

Section I: Personal Leadership

"It is Choice…
not Chance, that Determines Your Destiny"

Jean Nidetch's quote got me thinking about the events surrounding two different groups of people with whom I worked with in the last year promoting this article on Choice. The first involved several conversations with people who were talking about how they had let chance govern their career choices and how they now were struggling to make their own choices about where their careers would go from here. The second was several graduate students caught turning in papers as their own when they had, in fact, purchased them online. The first group had the opportunity to choose but couldn't. The second group had the opportunity to choose and chose poorly. It had me thinking, why are these choices so difficult?

Alfred Montepart once said, "Nobody ever did, or ever will, escape the consequences of his choices." Being an effective leader in today's global business environment requires a multitude of daily choices and every one of them has consequences. Granted, many of the consequences will be of the low to medium risk variety. However, some choices will carry consequences that may be unpopular, risky or difficult to understand. What they should not be is hard to live with. Let's go back to our two situations and see what leaders can learn from them.

Sustainable leadership does not leave success to chance. These leaders create visions, craft strategies to compete effectively and execute goal-based decisions to lead themselves and their businesses. They do not allow themselves to "wait-and-see" when the choices become difficult or when it is easier to go-with-the-flow.

Much is written on integrity and ethics as an issue for leaders in today's environment. I read an article of a ghostwriter who wrote papers for students from undergraduate to doctoral level, from teachers to seminarians and all walks of life in between. Those buying the papers knew of the wrong and consciously chose the unethical path.

Section I: Personal Leadership

Of concern is the rationalization that the ends justify the means; somehow, making unethical choices are justified on that premise. Effective leaders make their choices based on values that align with the vision for themselves and their businesses.

Every choice we make comes with its own set of consequences. Effective leaders understand this and consistently choose the harder right over the easier wrong when the situation calls for a choice to be made.

How much of your success is being left to chance?

Choose Wisely and Lead Well!

Section I: Personal Leadership

"Leaders Read!"

This statement succinctly states one of the key tenets to sustainable leadership. A longer version attributed to Thucydides goes, "The state which separates its scholars from its warriors will have its thinking done by cowards and its fighting done by fools." In other words, leaders at all levels must not only know the skills of their craft but also how and when to use those skills to achieve sustainable success.

Any chance I get, I take the opportunity to help leaders understand the value of leading from a position of knowledge versus an information-based position. The difference is in the context and meaning of knowledge. We live in a very information-rich world thanks in large part to technology. However, technology does not yet put that information into the context of the moment it is needed to make an informed decision. Leaders, themselves, must do that often with less than all the information needed to make the optimal decision.

So how do leaders put themselves in a position to process the magnitude of information to make knowledge-based decisions? Very simply, they acknowledge the value of being a life-long learner and execute accordingly. Life-long learners fall into two categories. There are those who learn because they have to and those who learn because they want to. The former is looking to address short-term issues such as dealing with new technologies or industry regulations. This leader is motivated by necessity. The latter is looking to fulfill an internal motivation to have knowledge of information that may or may not have value to them at the moment. These leaders tend to be motivated by possibility. Great leaders are focused on both.

Section I: Personal Leadership

Leadership learning occurs both formally and informally. Formal training, coaching and other structured learning opportunities should be an ongoing part of a leader's personal development plan. Personal development also includes informal opportunities such as reading, listening or viewing industry-specific and general-subject materials. Books, magazines, blogs, webinars and podcasts provide an excellent way to expand one's knowledge base.

Whether formal or informal learning, the crucial two questions to ask during and after each opportunity are:

1. How does this new information help create or enhance my competitive advantage?
2. How does this new information identify a potential competitive disadvantage?

Where is your Knowledge coming from?

Lead Well!

Section I: Personal Leadership

"If You Don't Like Change...
You're Going to Like Irrelevance Even Less"

One of the most frequent questions I ask business leaders, non-profit leaders and entrepreneurs is, "What makes your business unique and/or relevant in your market?" Regardless of the initial answer, the follow-up question is always the same, "How do you know?" These sets of questions are crucial for every leader to understand and embrace lest they fall victim to the condition General Eric Shinseki, former Chief of Staff of the Army spoke of in the opening quote.

So how do leaders stay relevant in a world of constant and seemingly spontaneous change? In my experience, there are three core areas every leader must master in order to stay relevant enough to be successful and sustainable leaders. The three areas are categorically: Attitude, Behavior and Skills & Knowledge.

The prevailing Attitude for relevance is one of continuously challenging the status quo. Those who know me and have worked with me know I personally hold steady to an evolutionary change every six months. I have a fundamental belief that if you are doing the same thing for longer than six months, someone else is already working on a way to do it better! This attitude is re-enforced by routinely asking myself variations of two basic questions, "What if...?" and "Why not...?" The answers keep me relevant!

Behaviorally, there are two actions keeping leaders relevant: Experimentation and Engagement. Some level of experimentation is a natural next step to the six-month mind-set from the previous paragraph. Experimentation allows you to challenge the status quo in a meaningful way to stay better informed around risk. Engagement is constant, always moving forward, even if you do not completely understand the impact.

Section I: Personal Leadership

Having the skills and knowledge to remain relevant can be summed up in one's ability to learn, unlearn and re-learn. Several years ago, I read 90% of what we know about how the human brain works we only learned in the last 11 years. It implies much of what we thought we knew about why we do what we do, we now have to re-learn. Emotional Intelligence in Leadership Development is a great example. Leaders must fully understand the roles of emotions in effective leadership, which may require unlearning old habits and re-learning new habits for sustainable success and relevance.

"Change is Constant, Growth is Not." We must constantly evolve to continue to grow.

How are you relevant and how do you know?

Lead Well!

Section I: Personal Leadership

"You Can't Talk Yourself Out of a Problem...
You Behaved Yourself Into"

The topic of choices and effective decision-making is consistently reinforced by the seemingly endless headlines highlighting poor choices and decisions in politics, entertainment, business and professional sports. Worse, the sideshow that becomes the attempts to apologize and/or explain the choices and decisions is what prompted this article's title, credited to Stephen Covey, author of 7 Habits of Highly Effective People. So what does it take to make an effective leadership decision?

One of the most critical elements in effective decision-making comes from the decision-maker's perspective in the decision. Without the proper perspective, or frame of reference, what appears to be a good decision from one perspective turns out not to be from the perspective of others on the receiving end of the decision.

An easy example from my own experience involves workforce reductions. If the perspective is to reduce expenses to a given number, the decision will likely yield the reduction of the highest paid associates. If the perspective is to manage through the tough period and leave the business able to grow beyond it, then the decision will yield the reduction of a different set of associates, possibly even more actual people than the first.

An effective way to change your frame of reference is to view the decision from the perspective of the future outcome. If we make a decision now and look back from the point of resolution, was this the best decision? Is there a better decision and, if so, what does it look like? Looking at the workforce reduction example above from this perspective, the frame of reference from the desired outcome helped me achieve the most effective decision.

Section I: Personal Leadership

Perspective gives leaders the backdrop to communicate their decisions to their stakeholders. As we read about behaviors of politicians, professional athletes and magazine editors, to name a few, it is their perspective that helps our understanding of their decisions.

How are you talking about the decisions you've behaved yourself into?

Lead Well!

Section 1: Personal Leadership

"This accountability crap is for the birds...
However, without it I would never get anything done"

This was an actual quote from a client of mine. They were going through a dramatic change in their business and recognized the value of accountability, no matter how painful it might be. It also reminded me how crucial it is for leaders to hold themselves, and those around them, accountable in order to achieve sustainable success.

In their 2012 book Challenging Coaching, consultants John Blakely and Ian Day suggest accountability falls into three major categories: Personal Accountability, which focuses on one's personal values, beliefs and attitudes that drive them toward action; Interpersonal Accountability, which focuses on common goals, responsibility and shared work; and Organizational Accountability, which focuses on standards, norms and measurements that apply to the entire organizational system. Let's explore each one a little deeper.

- **Personal Accountability –** accountability in general starts here! What we believe, we think, and what we think, we do. It stands to reason then that being accountable for our behavior is a reflection of how accountable we are to our own attitudes. If those attitudes are out of integrity or alignment with expectations, personal goal setting and achievement must become the norm.

- **Interpersonal Accountability –** accountability between people is built on the power of one's word. When we give our word to another, our actions must follow suit or we are out of integrity. No one likes to admit they are not working with integrity, but every time our actions do not match our words, that is exactly what is happening.

- ✓ **Organizational Accountability** – in an environment where multiple responsibilities, priorities and expectations exist across an organization, it is easy for organizational goals to be at cross-purposes with each other. How does the business align itself across the entire organization so people feel accountable to the entire mission, not just responsible for their part of the mission?

This last point is especially useful in the discussion of accountability. One's responsibilities are usually outlined in job descriptions, process flows or other systemic documents identifying what needs to get done by whom. Accountability is an attitude that transcends just one's responsibilities to ensure the team/business/organization becomes what their Vision invokes.

Alfred Montapert once said, "Nobody ever did, or ever will, escape the consequences of his choices."

How are you holding yourself accountable to your choices?

Lead Well!

Section 2:

Leadership Relationships

"People buy into the leader before they buy into the vision." ~ John Maxwell

Once we have a heightened sense of self-awareness, we can effectively lead others. Effective leaders know the importance of establishing and nurturing relationships with their most precious assets: their people! Collaboration is a crucial tool for successful lifelong leaders.

Section 2: Leadership Relationships

Are you aligned with your customer's business…
and how do you know?

The principles of the Business Alignment Maturity Model (see Appendix B) can be applied both internally and externally to your business. Internally, everything within our business must be in sync, or aligned to produce superior results. Here I will focus on the external view of Business Alignment and how it applies to your customers, suppliers, distributors and anyone else outside your business you depend on for your success.

For the moment, let's focus on your customers. Every customer you have, whether another business or a consumer, has a purpose and/or strategy behind their buying decisions. Their drive to succeed brought them to you. A business customer may have a more deliberate and pronounced Strategy, Structure and Goals where these may be more implied, though still exist, for the consumer customer. In other words, all customers are looking for alignment on some level when they come to you.

So where do you fit in their alignment process? Are you directly helping them solve their Goals or are you directly helping them achieve their Strategy and Vision? For the readers who do business with other businesses, look at your 5 largest customers and place your services and products in their business alignment process. Were you working on a project to achieve a tactical objective or was it tied to a strategic goal? Think of it as the difference between being a vendor or a strategic partner. In the consumer business, think of it as the difference between a single order and repeat business.

This idea is also valuable to you in relationships with your own vendors and/or partners. I recall a first time meeting with a supplier to discuss a new application. The first question the CEO asked me was "What is your Vision?" I knew immediately I was speaking with a leader who understood business alignment and where she wanted her company to participate in it. As I've outsourced parts of my business operations, I discussed my Vision with each supplier to ensure I am working with people who want my business and not just my order!

Section 2: Leadership Relationships

This idea of external business alignment is the basic foundation to building loyal relationships with customers, suppliers, distributors and all those who are instrumental in your success in today's business environment.

If I were to speak to your largest client, where would they place you in their alignment process and how would you know?

Lead Well!

Section 2: Leadership Relationships

"The best preparation for tomorrow...
is to do today's work superbly well"

These words of wisdom from Sir William Osler are timely on two levels. First, many of you are personally and/or professionally preparing for tomorrow – planning your goals for next week, month, quarter, year or beyond. Secondly, doing today's work superbly well speaks to, among other things, making every interaction with your customers a Moment of Truth. During this most recent economic recovery, moments of truth are significant to every business owner, corporate leader and non-profit leader who recognizes the importance of loyal customers and donors.

So what is a loyal customer? In my experience with many customer-facing positions in business services and non-profit organizations, I see the following traits as indicative of loyal customers compared to the satisfied customers we have traditionally sought.

- A loyal customer will proactively tell others about your service to others. A satisfied customer will tell others if you ask – maybe.

- A loyal customer will buy from you over and over again because you make it a no-brainer to do so. A satisfied customer will buy again – if it is convenient.

- A loyal customer is loyal because you continuously and routinely exceed their expectations. A satisfied customer has their expectations met - sometimes.

- A loyal customer is looking for, and gets, solutions to their business issues. A satisfied customer buys your products.

I recently came across an example of how inattention to moments of truth (points of connection) can negatively impact customer loyalty. Incidentally, I heard this story from multiple sources at unrelated events amplifying the impact. As a result of an acquisition, a computer retailer with local brick and mortar presence continues to advertise their services via the web. The consumer electronics company that purchased them markets the same products in the physical location at different prices, refusing to acknowledge the differences and failing to provide long time customers a consistent solution, only excuses.

Section 2: Leadership Relationships

Because loyal customers typically represent less than 20% of your total customer base, on average, the remaining customers represent an opportunity for both you AND your competitors. The opportunity is yours when you create and align your moments of truth to create a consistent value-based experience for your customers. However, the advantage goes to your competitors when you fail to provide consistent value and create a void in customer expectations. In the story above, leaders of the parent company created an environment where customers are now thinking about alternatives.

As you prepare for the future, to whom are you giving the advantage?

Lead Well!

Section 2: Leadership Relationships

We Will Do That For You...
Followed by a Firm Handshake

One of my favorite gifts from my sons is a sculpture of a handshake. They know I highly value the handshake as a symbol of the right kind of leader to be. It is no accident that it is part of the RPC Leadership Associates, Inc. brand. While difficult to locate the exact origin of the handshake, we can easily trace its history back as far as medieval times when knights and royalty would shake as a gesture to let the other know there were no weapons present. In other words, it was a sign of trust. It is trust with which we as a culture continue to struggle today.

We seldom go a day without seeing a headline or a story related to trust, typically a displayed lack of it. Whether in business, politics or sports, headlines conjure up images of broken trust between those men and women and the people who helped them succeed in the first place. So I believe it is here we should begin our discussion of trust by looking at what it means to have a meaningful relationship as a leader.

If we look at the buying process used by many in business for making a value-based decision, we find it begins with the first thing people buy – you! The strength of the relationship establishes the trust building process. Building trust is much like saving money in a piggy bank. Every moment of truth, every interaction with another person and every transaction in a relationship help build the trust bank account. When leaders look for trust in relationships with their teams, the first place they need to look is in the mirror. Are you the type of leader who is trustworthy? I spoke recently of self-awareness as the authentic leader's greatest tool. This is crucial as it helps a leader's ability to leverage candor and empathy as crucial elements to building trust. If people in an organization trust their leader as a person, they stand a much better chance of trusting their organization as a whole. Recent Gallup polls suggest only 30% of employees are fully engaged in their organization. What organization in this day and age can afford to have 30% engagement? Yet, by disregarding the very elements that build trust within the culture of their organization, they may as well hang a sign outside their door stating "Employee Engagement Doesn't Matter Here."

Section 2: Leadership Relationships

Finally, a fitting quote from David Armistead I often use, "Trust each other again and again. When the trust level gets high enough, people transcend apparent limits, discovering new and awesome abilities for which they were previously unaware." Are the trust levels in your organization high enough? Are you ready to discover new abilities in your organization to which you are now unaware?

What undiscovered new abilities are you still unaware due to your level of trust?

Lead Well!

Section 2: Leadership Relationships

"Lead, Follow...
or Get Out Of The Way"

This well-known quote from Thomas Paine serves as the basis for the Leadership Development component of the Total Leadership Process (Appendix B). Thomas Paine has been called the Voice of the Common Man and as such serves as a backdrop for the People aspect of Total Leadership. Purpose is the foundation of Total Leadership revealing itself through the organization's Vision and Strategy. The People aspect of Total Leadership looks at the organizational development processes organizations use to determine who can communicate the strategic objectives, execute those strategic objectives and provide feedback on progress made on the strategic objectives. In other words, how are organizations developing leaders at all levels of the organization?

In today's competitive, turbulent, fast-moving economy, developing the right leaders is imperative for survival of the business, whether for-profit or not-for-profit. As previous strategic assumptions likely will not work in our current economy, so too are the attitudes and methods traditionally used to develop leaders called into question. Effective leadership is no longer about possessing certain personal characteristics but about setting goals and achieving desired results.

So what does this mean exactly? It means we have to get beyond the assumption if you grow certain leadership qualities in people they will somehow positively impact operational results. Too much time, money and energy are wasted creating a yardstick of designated leadership characteristics only to find they are yesterday's news based on the fast changing external and internal forces for change all organizations face. It becomes a journey of hope no more effective in today's market than the "Field of Dreams" (build it and they will come) business strategy.

The solution is about defining and justifying leadership development on the tangible outcomes it is intended to produce. It drives a strategy focused on the desired results and then grows and develops the people (and processes) to realize those results. As Peter Drucker so aptly stated, "Leadership is all about the Results."

Section 2: Leadership Relationships

The challenge with this solution is it assumes the People development process throughout any organization is aligned to its Purpose. Is the Leadership Development process in your organization linked to the Vision and Strategy so when the Strategy adjusts to economic changes your organization automatically adjusts the leadership development to leverage new skills and deliver new results?

If not, are these leaders really leading or are they just in the way?

Lead Well!

Section 2: Leadership Relationships

"Customer Satisfaction is Worthless...
Customer Loyalty is Priceless"

This often quoted title from Jeffrey Gitomer's book sets the stage for the Profit component of the Total Leadership Model (Appendix B). Much is written about the general differences between satisfied customers and loyal customers. However, the real question becomes "How is Customer Loyalty a competitive advantage?"

Customers generate revenue, loyal customers generate profit. When I was leading corporate organizations, our customer and sales support teams worked closely alongside our sales teams. It was a relationship not always obvious or easy to manage, but one I always insisted on nonetheless. While I was interested in the initial sale to a new client, I was even more interested in the second, third, fourth, ad infinitim sales. Why? Because I knew how important the follow-on sales were to profitability and creating emotional relationships with our customers. In industries where the core products and services are commoditized, it was the power of points of connection, or "Moments of Truth," that drove ongoing loyalty within our customer base. Studies show as little as a 5% increase in customer loyalty can drive an increase in profits from 25% to over 80%. To highlight the power of moments of truth, another study showed that if an organization's employees were 100% engaged, they would see a 70% increase in customer loyalty. Why is this significant? As mentioned before, a recent Gallup Poll showed an average employee engagement level of 30%. Said differently, 70% of employees are disengaged, creating an untenable gap in the ability to create powerful points of connection with their customer base and causing a direct drain on profits!

But who or what are we loyal to? We know when we engage in the Buying/Selling process, buyers look to buy you first before they look at your company or your products. They are looking to establish the first of the three components necessary to developing customer loyalty – trust.

Section 2: Leadership Relationships

Whether it is you, the entrepreneur, you, the corporate leader, or you, the non-profit leader, prospective customers and donors are first and foremost looking to see if they trust you! What is their first impression of you, your brand, your office or your website? What are others saying about you? These moments of truth become the catalyst to creating a consistent experience creating the second component of loyalty – a strong emotional tie with the customer. The third component of customer loyalty is using empathy to continuously and consistently meet and/or exceed an ever-increasing level of expectation in today's business environment. It is the customer's experience with you that counts. Peter Drucker once said, "Quality in a Service or Product is not what you put into it. It is what the Client or Customer gets out of it."

Do your customers find your products or services worthless or priceless and how do you know?

Lead Well!

Section 2: Leadership Relationships

Resentment is like drinking poison...
and waiting for the other person to die

How many times do we find ourselves trying to blame someone or something else for our own issues and challenges? It is human nature to get defensive when we find ourselves stuck or moving in a direction we did not want. Leaders at all levels become paralyzed from achieving their goals by the notion that they would be more successful if only someone else or something else would change. Their own attitudes are the greatest obstacles to success!

Attitudes are habits of thought and, as such, have similar characteristics of any habit we wish to change. Changing an attitude requires us to replace the attitude that works against us like: "If only we had more resources" or "If only they would change." An effective goal achievement process is crucial to making this happen.

An effective goal achievement process enables new habits of thought by replacing the old habits and leads to more successful leadership attitudes. While most goal setting processes identify action steps to achieve a stated goal, a goal achievement process identifies the reasons why the goal is important and what the potential obstacles to achieving that goal are. By identifying why the goal is important and what could potentially derail the goal, a different set of action steps are created that allow for a higher degree of success. A higher level of success replaces the old attitudes in the previous paragraph with ones like: "How will we achieve our goal with what I have available?" or "How can we think of this issue differently that allows us to be successful?"

A new and different mindset or attitude now allows us to think about an issue or challenge in a much different way. When I was a new Vice President of Client Care, it became evident to me one of the missing elements to success was an effective training and development program for the organization. It would have been easy to blame the lack of a training and development budget and take no more action to remedy the situation. However, that would be like drinking the poison and waiting for the other person to die.

Section 2: Leadership Relationships

Instead, I tapped into my network and found resources willing to assist us with little or no budget. A former director of mine provided leadership training for the management team. Another friend of mine created a new leadership curriculum based on the lessons we learned at West Point. Our management team volunteered to be a pilot group allowing us to receive top-notch leadership training for free.

The lesson in the story is not about getting training on a shoestring budget, it is about the attitude that looks for creative and innovative ways to overcome obstacles versus finding blame for not succeeding.

What poisonous attitude is holding you back from your success?

Lead Well!

Section 2: Leadership Relationships

Information is Knowing a Tomato is a Fruit...
Knowledge is Knowing not to put it in a Fruit Salad

In other parts of this book, we discuss the relationship between Information (organized data) and Knowledge (information in context). I bring it up again not to highlight the contents of a fruit salad, but to highlight a much more crucial issue for leaders – timely decision-making. In my work with leaders, we describe the first two steps in the decision-making process as 1) Identify the Issue and 2) Gather and Analyze Information. The decision-maker must properly define the scope of the problem, situation or challenge in enough detail to create tangible alternatives. They must also gather the right amount of the right information to make a knowledgeable decision.

Information overload is not a new challenge. Lucius Annaeus Seneca was a Senator and Advisor under Nero in the early part of his reign. Seneca was a prolific letter writer whose thoughts, insights and convictions were well read throughout the literate Roman Empire. Even in his day, he noted the issue with connectedness by observing, "the danger of allowing others – not just friends and colleagues, but the masses – to exert too much influence on one's thinking." Without mentioning these words were written around the time of Christ, you could easily assume they were written recently.

To the decision-maker, it is no longer just a task to find the relevant information to use but to weed out and discard the unnecessary information and do it at the speed of competition. This is no easy task considering the amount of information available to us doubles every 9 – 10 minutes (depending on which study you read). The proliferation of Twitter, blogs, Facebook and texting contributes to this informational tsunami. The task is further compounded by having to analyze increasingly shorter and more cryptic information (Twitter reports over 2 billion tweets a month) while at the same time ensuring it is factually correct.

Section 2: Leadership Relationships

As I look at the impact this phenomenon has on our decision-making process as leaders, I see less contingency planning due to the instantaneous nature of technology and less reflection on the meaning of information to create sustainable knowledge. Even the aforementioned Seneca wrote, "Elite, literate Romans were discovering the great paradox of information: the more of it that is available, the harder it is to be truly knowledgeable. It was impossible to process it all in a thoughtful way."

As leaders striving to make effective knowledgeable decisions about your business, how many tomatoes are in your fruit salad?

Lead Well!

Section 2: Leadership Relationships

"Baby Boomers are immigrants...
to the world that Gen X and Yers are born into"

This quote is from the January 2011 issue of FastCompany.com addressing the leadership changes at Google. In the article, the author uses the leadership arrangement at the search company as an example of what he calls "Bi-Leadership—Bi-Generational, Boomer, Gen-X, Gen-Y management." It also provides a great backdrop for a topic every leader today must understand – generational diversity.

As we look at today's business landscape, we see four generations (and a fifth around the corner) in the workplace. It is in understanding how each generation has a different view of the world and how each communicates in unique ways that makes managing the different generations a challenge for today's leaders. While the Traditionalists (those 65 years old and over) continue in the workforce, their numbers are dwindling, especially as the economy recovers. And while you may have already heard of Generation Z (those just turning 14 years old), they are only now beginning to enter the workforce. For purposes of this article and the next, a two-part series, we will focus on the other three generations - Baby Boomers, Generation X and Generation Y.

Baby Boomers are the generation born between 1946 and 1964. They were influenced by the Cold War, the Civil Rights Movement, the Watergate Scandal and Woodstock. As a result, these roughly 76M people value hard work to get ahead, competition, teamwork and face-to-face communications.

The next generation, Generation X, was born between 1965 and 1981. They were influenced by recession and high unemployment so they came to value entrepreneurship and creativity. These approximately 46M people also value having greater access to information and feedback than their predecessors.

Section 2: Leadership Relationships

Generation Y, or Millenials, were born between 1982 and 2005 (this may vary depending on the study). This is the largest generation of the three totaling just over 80M people by some estimates. Their major influences were technology and growing up with "helicopter parents" and "snowplow parents." Consequently, as a generation, they value positive reinforcement (lots of it), structure, technology and autonomy.

With this level of disparity in the workplace, leaders must understand what each generation brings to the organization. They must also know how to bridge the gaps between them to achieve the organization's desired results.

How might your own generational perceptions impact your ability to build bridges between generations?

Lead Well!

Section 2: Leadership Relationships

Why should we care about...
four generations in the workplace?

In the previous article, we spoke of the four generations (Traditionalist, Baby Boomers, Generation X and Generation Y) currently in the workplace and some of their prevailing influences. Now we will look closer at the unique ways leaders can retain, motivate and effectively lead each of these generations individually and collectively as members of the same team.

Generally speaking, older generations perceive the younger generation's work ethics as lacking in some way compared to theirs. In truth, each generation believes their work ethic is fine leading to the leader's challenge – how to get past the perceptions. The place to start is a better understanding of how each prevailing generation (Boomers, Gen X and Gen Y) is motivated and best managed to avoid losing the talent they bring to the organization.

Baby Boomers want to be appreciated for the experience and knowledge they bring to an organization. While they may resist change, they generally do so out of dedication to the organization, which is very important to them. Giving them opportunities to mentor is a great way to show you respect their contributions. I would take this further and create a reverse-mentoring process where the Boomers mentor the younger generations who, in turn, mentor the Boomers on skills to help them keep up with the pace of business.

Generation X, on the other hand, is looking for more flexible schedules and the opportunity to be problem-solvers. After all, this is the latchkey generation whose Boomer parents both worked so they had to fend for themselves growing up. They typically do not need to be micro-managed but do crave feedback from their leaders.

Section 2: Leadership Relationships

Leading Generation Y requires yet another set of leadership expectations. Gen Y needs structure and stability, which means feedback, feedback and more feedback. They are very cause-oriented and socially conscious which is key for organizations looking for sustainability solutions. Authenticity and transparency also matter to a generation that is used to finding whatever they need or want through technology. However, they will likely need their leader's help with effective communications and problem solving for the very same reason.

A word of caution, these generalizations are just that – generalizations and do not define individuals as such. Successful leaders move beyond the perceptions and generalizations to tap the personal power of each individual they lead.

How well do you know everyone on your team?

Lead Well!

Section 2: Leadership Relationships

"Peace is not the absence of conflict...
But the presence of creative alternatives
for responding to conflict"

I am reminded of these words from Dorothy Thompson every Fourth of July, and they seem an appropriate introduction to this article's leadership topic – Managing Conflict. Much like our founding fathers managed conflict to achieve independence, so, too, must today's leaders be prepared to manage conflict in their organizations to achieve desired results. I often define Conflict as an interaction between interdependent parties who perceive incompatible goals or interference from others in achieving their goals. When managing conflict, leaders should pay close attention to the level of interdependence between the parties involved and the foundation of each other's perceptions. Establishing this level of interdependence helps leaders address the conflict in the context of the relationships involved. Addressing the perceptions by all parties enables leaders to understand the issues in the context of the facts of the conflict.

Effective communication is the root of these two challenges. Communication contributes to both the cause and the cure of conflict. Conflict typically shows itself in the absence of effective communication, creating misperceptions and information vacuums. Effective communication is a key catalyst to cure a conflict with the ability to bring parties together to understand the importance of the interdependent relationships, fill information voids and reset perceptions to their proper levels. A Leader's ability to step into any conflict situation and effectively communicate to all parties can be the difference between success and failure, but not all Leaders are the same and not all Leaders manage conflict the same way.

Ralph H. Kilmann and Kenneth W. Thomas identified 5 specific Conflict Management styles based on their research in the early '70's. The five styles are based on how aggressively one pursues their own goals (Assertiveness) against how aggressively they cooperate with the other parties in the conflict (Cooperativeness).

- ✔ Avoidance – Low Assertiveness, Low Cooperativeness
- ✔ Accommodation – Low Assertiveness, High Cooperativeness

Section 2: Leadership Relationships

- ✓ Compromise – Medium Assertiveness, Medium Cooperativeness
- ✓ Competition – High Assertiveness, Low Cooperativeness
- ✓ Collaboration – High Assertiveness, High Cooperativeness

Each style carries with it a unique set of skills, both communication and others, which may or may not be the Leader's strength.

At no point have we discussed eliminating conflict. As leaders, we must all recognize conflict will always exist and learn to effectively manage it through effective communication and awareness of our natural management style.

How are you achieving Peace in your organization?

Lead Well!

Section 2: Leadership Relationships

"Preach Always...
Sometimes Use Words"

We have all heard the phrase "Practice What You Preach" at some point in our lives. There is even a variation that goes "Preach What You Practice." The underlying theme is the effective combination of Preaching and Practice. However, Preaching does not always mean words are involved.

What do people see from your actions? What are you preaching without saying anything? We often forget that every move we make as leaders is under some level of scrutiny. People are watching and judging based on their perception of what a leader should do, or not do. Internally, followers are deciding how much they are going to follow based on what they see. Externally, customers are deciding if they trust and want to do business based on what they see. Constant scrutiny without saying a word!

However, when we do speak and act, the ante increases. Our words and actions reflect directly onto our integrity. While integrity has many definitions, the one I like the most in this context is someone "having ethical integrity to the extent that the individual's actions, beliefs, methods, measures and principles all derive from a single core group of values." My own short version is: someone's Beliefs, Words and Actions all tell the same story.

When we speak and act, people are not only judging our words and actions against their own set of values and beliefs, they are also judging the congruence between our own words and our own actions. Anyone in the public eye can vouch for the challenge that might present. We can likely all tell a story or two about a leader in our past or present who made a passionate appeal with their words to do certain things to advance the business. That same person then either did nothing or their actions ran contrary to the words they spoke. This mismatch made them out of integrity and eroded their value in the eyes of those who were impacted by the integrity breach. That level of integrity breach is difficult, at best, to recover from.

Section 2: Leadership Relationships

"Lead by Example" is a phrase we all have heard many times throughout our careers. In this day and age of transparency and technology that can literally capture our every move, it is even more important that we preserve our integrity and ensure our actions and words are telling the same story.

What are you silently preaching loudly?

Lead Well!

Section 2: Leadership Relationships

"Leadership is not wielding Authority ... it's Empowering People"

As I reflected on my coaching activity over the last several years, I realized much of my time was spent with a collective group representing a crucial leadership component in any organization - middle management. I am referring to those Senior Managers and Directors who are typically one or two levels removed from the front lines of the business as well as several layers removed from the boardroom. Yet, to be successful, they keep an eye on, and understand the activities of, both ends of the spectrum. Based on recent experience, it is still as challenging as it was when I held similar positions in my own corporate career. The expression above from Becky Brodin is a reminder of an integral part of the being a successful middle management leader – Empowerment!

In my own experience, there are four distinct ways leaders in middle management can be effective either by empowering their teams or being empowered themselves to make the right decisions and achieve their desired results.

- ✔ Be the top when necessary. Being able to make decisions when needed without always having to "run it up the chain of command" is indicative of an empowered leader as well as a high performing organization.

- ✔ Be the bottom when necessary. Being able to filter and/or translate the volume of information that comes from senior leadership requires a current knowledge of what is important to their team and what is not.

- ✔ Be the facilitator when necessary. When issues cross the middle management leader's path, they become opportunities to facilitate a solution rather than solve the problem directly.

- ✔ Be the coach when necessary. Similar to facilitating, coaching helps individuals create their own solutions to issues with the support of the coaching leader.

Section 2: Leadership Relationships

When I work with leaders in middle management positions, I always explore empowerment on two levels. We look at the leader's level of empowerment with their own team as well as the level of empowerment they receive from their managers.

How much is empowerment contributing to your success as a leader?

Lead Well!

Section 2: Leadership Relationships

We are not Hard of Hearing…
We are Hard of Listening!

It's true! Most of us hear everything around us. We hear the familiar noises of our day (traffic, radio, family, etc.), and it reminds us of where we are and what we are doing. But are we truly listening to what we hear when it matters most and how do we know?

Jim Cathcart once said, "Listening is wanting to hear." The implication here is that listening is a choice, a choice to comprehend what is being heard. When I conduct Leadership Communications workshops, the topic of listening is always part of the agenda. Below are five ways a leader can choose to become a more effective listener.

- ✔ Take Time to Listen – It does take time to listen effectively as a discussion cut short due to distractions or interruptions will not yield its full value. This also means being in the moment both physically AND mentally. We all know that person who is looking at us but also looking through us as if they to want to be somewhere else – don't be that person.

- ✔ Be Attentive to the Speaker – When someone speaks to you, they do so because the topic is important to them. Even if their issue ranks lower on your importance scale, paying attention to them allows you to better formulate your own ideas as a leader. No leader can afford to be perceived as someone who does not care about his or her team because they are not attentive to what their team is saying. Yet we see it happen nearly every day!

- ✔ Listen with an Open Mind – I have learned much in my career by being attentive to people whose views with which I did not agree. If nothing else, it provides a more complete picture of the facts. In this day and age of too much information and not enough knowledge, listening with an open mind can level that imbalance

Section 2: Leadership Relationships

- ✓ Listen for Feelings – Emotional Intelligence is not new to the realm of leadership any more. It is a given that effective leaders leverage emotional intelligence as a success factor and do so because they can listen for feelings. They are not only listening to the words but are listening to how the words are spoken. Tone, hesitation, speed and pitch all contribute to understanding the feelings involved in the discussion.

- ✓ Listen for Retention – How many of us heard a great joke or story a few days ago and now have the opportunity to re-tell it and cannot remember a single word? In a leadership scenario, that lack of retention could be the difference between success and failure.

We define Effective Communications as the sender and receiver understanding the message in the same context. Active listening is a crucial component to successfully understanding what is being said, how it is being said and the meaning of what is being said.

If "Listening is wanting to hear," what would you like to hear?

Lead (and Listen) Well!

Section 2: Leadership Relationships

"The Right to Lead can only be earned…
and that takes time"

These words from John C. Maxwell provide the impetus for this leadership narrative. This topic comes up frequently in discussions with clients, students and even in the press. More specifically, it speaks to the power we have as leaders and our attitudes towards how we use that power.

The first thing successful leaders understand is they are never the judges of their own leadership. I liken the concept to how a business states the quality of their products and services. They rely on their customers to ensure the quality of their products and services are meeting and/or exceeding the customer's expectations. In like fashion, successful leaders understand the true nature of their leadership lies in their followers. Much like the Afghan proverb, "If you think you are leading and no one is following you, then you are only taking a walk," leaders earn their right to lead from their followers and leverage their own power to do so.

Power for leaders is defined in two ways. It can show itself as Positional Thinking, or the attitude that one's title and position defines their leadership. While one's position may define one's scope of responsibility, it will never fully define successful leadership. That requires another form of power called Persuasive Thinking or Personal Power.

Personal Power is the power we have as individuals to influence others. More directly, influence is defined as others' behavioral response to one's (the leader's) exercise of power. It is through influence that followership occurs. We see this personal power show itself in several ways. We see it through:

- ✓ **Rational Persuasion –** making a logical case for action

- ✓ **Expert Power –** influence by virtue of one's expertise

- ✓ **Referent Power –** being the role-model others will emulate

- ✓ **Coalition Power –** being part of a larger circle of influence

Section 2: Leadership Relationships

When leaders influence followers, they tap into the followers' motivation to fully engage in the organizational mission and goals. Much has been written about the challenges of employee engagement in today's workforce and the large financial impact it has on the organization. The importance of fully leveraging personal power to achieve this level of engagement cannot be overstated.

Motivation is a choice by the follower, not the leader. In this context, we know successful leaders are not directly motivating their followers; rather, they influence their followers by earning their trust, giving them motivation to fully engage for sustainable success.

How are you earning the right to lead?

Lead Well!

Section 2: Leadership Relationships

"To Be a Better Leader...
Be a Better Person and Lead Naturally"

I came across these words many years ago and they are one of the key influences behind the RPC Leadership Associates, Inc. Vision of "Making Leadership a Way of Life." Far too many people rely solely on a class, a book or a workshop to become better leaders. What they fail to fully realize is the importance of understanding who they are as a foundation for effective leadership development.

So what do we mean by being a better person as a foundation for being a better leader? In a word, integrity! More specifically, personal integrity defined as our beliefs, our words and our actions all telling the same story. We all know people from our past or present who we know believe in one thing and say another, or those who say one thing and do another. These people are "out of integrity" as there exists disconnects between their beliefs, words and actions.

As a leader, our followers are looking for the integrity in our beliefs, words and actions, especially the latter two. Followers may not have a full understanding of our personal beliefs. However, they are very much attuned to our words and actions to see if they are, in fact, the same. If so, we can build a culture of trust between leaders and followers that is natural and authentic.

Section 2: Leadership Relationships

A client recently shared these words that I believe are relevant to this idea of personal integrity:

Watch your thoughts;

They become your words.

Watch your words;

They become your actions.

Watch your actions;

They become your habits.

Watch your habits;

They become your character.

Watch your character;

It becomes your destiny.

What will your leadership destiny be?

Lead Well!

Section 2: Leadership Relationships

"The Best Way to Find Out if You Can Trust Someone... Is to Trust Them"

Frequently, the subject of trust is the underlying theme in conversations with clients, graduate students and workshop participants. As I reflected on these conversations, it became apparent there are a good number of potential leaders waiting for others to make the first "trust" move. It is this contradiction that prompted the title quote above from Ernest Hemingway as the lead to this discussion of trust.

So how do we trust someone? While there are many ideas around this topic, my experience tells me there are two key elements to successfully trusting others - Integrity and Attitude.

Integrity occurs when our beliefs, actions and words all tell the same story. When we actually do what we say we are going to do, we engender trust in others. I have coached students and clients alike to pay little attention to the words of others but pay very close attention their actions. The more followers trust the leader's ability to "walk the talk," the more deposits they make into the "trust" account. Trust deposits are made in small increments, so it takes time to build a level of trust that is sustainable. Conversely, when the leader breaks the trust, essentially making a withdrawal from the "trust" account, it happens quickly and is on magnitudes of scale compared to deposits.

Attitude is the other dimension of trust I find represents successful leadership. I have always believed someone is trustworthy until they give me a reason to not trust them. It is an attitude that people see when we work together. Again, there are many reasons to not trust in business, politics, sports or society in general. However, believing society in general is untrustworthy is not fair to those who are. In instances where members of a team could not be trusted, the situation was dealt with quickly and decisively. Sustainable organizations need trust to succeed. Therefore, there can be no hesitation when dealing with a lack of trust.

Section 2: Leadership Relationships

David Armistead once said: "Trust each other again and again. When the trust level gets high enough, people transcend apparent limits, discovering new and awesome abilities for which they were previously unaware."

Therefore, true trust is a sustainable success multiplier. I often hear how trust exists in an organization based on how the organization works well together. My argument is: the absence of conflict does not equal the presence of trust! Trust must be an overt action by the leader, and it is the leader's responsibility to make the first move to establish a trusting culture through their integrity and attitude.

Who do you trust and, more importantly, who trusts you?

Lead Well!

Section 2: Leadership Relationships

"A mediocre leader tells…
A good leader explains. A superior leader demonstrates.
A great leader inspires others to see for themselves."

I took the liberty of taking Harvey Mackay's quote and substituting "leader" for the word "person" in the original quote. It struck me how the meaning remains intact and offers insights into the leaders we need to become in today's business environment.

A question I often ask in my practice is, "Why would someone follow you?" The question is intended to move the definition of effective leadership from the leader's perspective to that of the people who would follow them. The answers range from "I don't know" to full explanations of how desired results were achieved because their teams clearly understood the direction and expectations of the business and were given the resources to succeed as a team. These insightful answers come complete with examples and stories of how leadership played a role in helping the team see themselves as the key to success!

So how do you get from "I don't know" to telling stories of successful leadership? The secret is how well people are aligned to the Vision, Mission and Strategy of the organization. This implies, of course, the organization has these guiding statements along with a set of shared values that are consistently communicated in a way so that everyone understands both the words and the intent. It means I could walk up to anyone in the organization, ask, "How does what you do help the organization achieve its Vision and Strategy?" and I would get a clear answer.

These open-ended questions become the leader's primary communication tool to help their teams understand how they fit into the Strategy. Leaders must be comfortable with asking open-ended questions in every interaction with their teams. Questions beginning with "How" and "What" or even "Why" engage followers to be part of the discussion and see solutions in their own minds.

Section 2: Leadership Relationships

Another benefit to the leader, the better a leader is at asking open-ended questions, the better listener they become! Open-ended questions typically generate longer and more thoughtful answers so the opportunity to develop better listening skills is a great complement to engaging followers.

People follow leaders with a clear Vision and Strategy for the organization. They follow leaders who engage them physically, intellectually and emotionally to execute the Strategy. As a friend of mine recently posted on Facebook, "The Secret Of Success Is Figuring Out How To Make Other People Successful."

Why would someone follow you?

Lead Well!

Section 2: Leadership Relationships

People Hear Words...
but Think in Pictures

When we talk about successful leadership, we have to include the leader's ability to effectively communicate with the stakeholders of the business. Clients, employees, suppliers and investors are all examples of stakeholders who have an impact on the success of the business regardless of industry, size or tax status. The question is, when they hear the leader's words, is the mental picture one the leader wants them to have?

We define Effective Communications as the speaker and listener understanding the message in the same context. This means all parties understand the message based on what was overtly stated as well as what was implied. This is especially true for messages communicated to a large stakeholder audience or when the message itself relates to a complex topic and subject.

The challenge is evident in so many cases where I meet with leaders struggling with effectively communicating. Their first instinct is to ask, "Why don't they get it?" or " Why aren't they listening?" In fact, the responsibility for this breakdown lies more with the speaker than the listeners. As Andrew Grove, former CEO of Intel Corp. once said, "How well we communicate is determined not by how well we say things but by how well we are understood."

So how does a leader communicate effectively and paint the right mental picture in the minds of their listeners? In my experience, the answer is in how well they address both Content and Context.

- **Content is the Information leaders share and must be Simple, Relevant and Organized:**

  - Simple - words convey ideas with minimal jargon and multi-syllabic buzzwords.

  - Relevant - words focus on a central theme or point.

  - Organized - words move the listener from known facts to unknown ideas and from simple concepts to new, more complex ideas.

Section 2: Leadership Relationships

- **Context, where Information becomes Knowledge, is built on Purpose, Action and Feedback:**

  - Purpose - content relates to a greater Ideal or Vision helping the listener answer, "This is important because..."

  - Action - content invokes a Call to Action by the listener within the framework of the Purpose.

  - Feedback - content is fed back to the speaker to validate Purpose alignment and Action appropriateness.

As you speak your words, what pictures are your listeners creating in their minds?

Lead (and Communicate) Well!

Section 3:

Organizational Leadership

"The achievements of an organization are the results of the combined efforts of each individual." ~ Vince Lombardi

No matter how well the organization is stacked individually, the combined efforts must still generate desired results. Successful lifelong leadership is achieved by creating an environment where people can succeed individually AND collectively!

Section 3: Organizational Leadership

If the economy is not going back to what it was…
why are you still running your business the same way
it was back then?

In a networking event several years ago, I asked the assembled businesses if they thought the economy would revert back to the way it was 2 years ago. No one raised their hand. I then asked how many have changed their business model to account for that new reality. Only 4 or 5 out of 30 raised their hand. Leadership is about managing change, and there has been no more significant change requiring authentic leadership in recent history as now. Unfortunately, we see many businesses, large and small, not coping well with the changes needed to keep their businesses viable. A vast majority of companies will need to leverage their ability to change on their own and reach into the leadership tool kit for never before used tools.

Understanding how to manage change involves first recognizing that a change is needed. The skills and knowledge that brought your business to this point will not likely guarantee your success going forward. What are your customers asking for? What are your suppliers telling you? What are your own sales and operations people saying about their ability to succeed? What is your Vision? Under normal circumstances, a Vision is what would help direct the organization during times of change. Every business needs a sense of direction, and I would go so far as to suggest the reason many small and mid-sized businesses are stalled is the absence of a Vision.

It is not enough to just have a Vision. It must be communicated openly and frequently to the rest of the organization, to suppliers and to customers. Leadership during change requires a communication strategy second to none to ensure all organizations contributing to your business success are on the same page. However, this requires the business leader to be transparent and authentic.

Transparency requires the leader to be frank and honest about what is going on in the business and to effectively communicate where the business is going. Authenticity means being a leader those associated with the business can trust.

Section 3: Organizational Leadership

The leader during times of change and challenge must be credible, and the rules of what a credible leader is in this economy are uncompromising. You cannot be credible through taking a pill or getting a shot. You cannot gain it by submitting to a surgical procedure. You have to Believe It, Think It and Do It!

In my experience, there are two types of managers during times of challenge and change. The first are those who stall and wait for change to happen. The others are those who drive forward continuously with a purpose to achieve their Vision. The first types are victims and act accordingly. The second types are true leaders and are rewarded accordingly.

Which one are you?

Lead Well!

Section 3: Organizational Leadership

*"The art of progress is to preserve order amid change...
and to preserve change amid order"*

This quote by Alfred North Whitehead symbolizes the leadership challenge faced by business of all sizes and industries in today's competitive economic landscape. This quote implies there is careful balance required amidst change to maintain some measure of order in business organizations and plans while at the same time identifying and executing change strategies in order to achieve real progress. My experience suggests many businesses are doing one aspect of this process well but struggling to do the other and/or both to full effectiveness.

So how does today's leader manage order and change simultaneously? The answer lies in the business Strategy. Simply stated, your business Strategy dictates how your organization competes in its industry and markets. Having created strategies in large corporate, small entrepreneurial, mature and startup, for-profit and non-profit businesses, this definition of Strategy holds true universally. The strategy is a by-product of the leader(s) taking an objective and in-depth look at their external environment in order to create the Vision. It also holds the results of an unbiased view of the business's internal capabilities identified through a detailed SWOT (Strengths, Weaknesses, Opportunities and Threats) process or similar assessment process. The Strategy becomes a series of goal categories (also referred to as strategic objectives) determined to be critical to the business in a competitive environment.

Section 3: Organizational Leadership

It is not enough to have a Strategy as a standalone document. It must also link to both the business goals and vision to be effective in the context of creating real progress. Linking the Strategy to business goals is accomplished through creation of specific goals from each of the critical goal categories identified in the Strategy. This alignment typically represents managing order amid change in the opening quote. Just as important is the linkage of the Strategy to the vision of the business. This alignment ensures the critical goal categories are relevant to the overall direction of the business and/or organization. If you cannot articulate clear alignment between current strategic objectives and where the business is going, the competitive markets will take the business where they want it to go. In essence, without direction (read: control), any road will look like a valid one! This also represents the managing change amid order element of the opening quote.

Organizational movement can just happen and be confused for progress. Real progress requires a Strategy that is both linked to the vision and the specific goals of the business to be effective. There are two types of leaders during times of challenge and change. The first are those who are busy managing order. The second types are creating real progress!

Which one are you?

Lead Well!

Section 3: Organizational Leadership

"Leadership is responsible for 94% of quality problems...
so it is leadership's responsibility to help people work smarter,
not harder"

These words by W. Edwards Deming are a call to action for today's leaders to help them focus on the right business goals in order to execute their business strategies. You may recall Deming as the statistician who made popular the Plan-Do-Check-Act Cycle and is considered the father of modern quality control. It is also relevant we consider his thoughts as today's leaders address the challenges of achieving their business strategies in an unstable economy, an uncertain regulatory environment and untapped globalization.

Against this backdrop are elements of the alignment process that fall between Strategy and Goals in the Business Alignment Maturity Model (see Appendix B).). These layers often go unnoticed and unattended by leaders until it is far too late. The Structure layer prompts leaders to look at their People, Processes and Technology to ensure these elements directly support the prevailing business Strategy. This is universally true whether applied to large corporate business models or small or mid-sized entrepreneurial ventures. The focus for this discussion is the Process component in the Structure layer of the Model.

Specifically addressing the business processes as part of the structure alignment takes us back to the opening quote. If processes do not align to the core strategy, then achieving desired results is next to impossible. It is up to business leadership to make that happen.

As Dr. H. James Harrington stated in his book Business Process Improvement in the section devoted specifically to CEOs, "The biggest opportunity you have to improve the bottom line comes from improving your business processes." Again, this may seem as though it is geared towards larger organizations. However, it is just as applicable to medium and small businesses managing their employees, vendors and suppliers as well as non-profit organizations managing their organizations of volunteers and staff.

Section 3: Organizational Leadership

In today's business environment, regardless of whether you are an entrepreneur or a corporate president/CEO, Structure dictates your business success. Leadership is what ties them to the Strategy and Goals.

How is your Structure supporting your Strategy?

Lead Well!

Section 3: Organizational Leadership

Are we there yet?

How many times have we heard that refrain from those around us when their impatience got the best of them? Or maybe we've said it ourselves in different situations for the same reason. In most cases, it is said because there is no sense of time or speed relative to correct expectations of arrival.

In the business sense, whether for-profit or non-profit, we will at some point find ourselves compiling data telling us how well our business has performed over the last business cycle (month, quarter, half-year). Or are we? This article focuses on the all-important role of measurements as a crucial element of effective business alignment. We are talking about what we regularly measure as well as how we measure what we do in order to make informed business decisions.

The first place to start is to be clear on what we are capturing and the usefulness of what we capture. There are essentially 4 levels of "stuff" we measure: Data, Information, Knowledge and Wisdom, sometimes referred to as the DIKW Hierarchy. Like many topics in and around leadership, much has been written about these 4 elements, so I am going to focus on the salient points of each.

- **Data** is what we measure directly. It is raw in nature and is the least useful element to making the level of business decisions we need to run our business.

- **Information** is organized Data. In a practical sense, this means we import all the available data into a spreadsheet or database and sort or index the data to make it more useful for making a meaningful business decision.

Section 3: Organizational Leadership

- ✔ **Knowledge** is Information in context. While Information is useful for many business related decisions, its usefulness is limited without the context around the Information gathered. Knowledge allows us to make informed strategic decisions.

- ✔ **Wisdom** is Knowledge over time. When we apply Knowledge over time, we create an environment in which the learning of the organization is exponential due to the richness and usefulness of each decision, leading to even more useful outcomes.

As an example, Organization A and Organization B captured data from expense reduction efforts and compiled the data in a spreadsheet to see if they reduced their expenses to meet a specific financial target. However, Organization B went one step further to ensure there were minimal reductions in areas critical to its long term Strategy with the balance coming from less critical parts of the business. Organization A made their decisions based on information while Organization B made knowledge-based strategic decisions and did not lose sight of the contextual impact of their decision.

Which organization do you work for?

Lead Well!

Section 3: Organizational Leadership

*41% of small businesses are paying their employees...
just to show up at work!*

That is, they are not held to any performance standard that somehow ties results of their responsibilities to their paycheck. According to a survey released in 2009 by George S. May International, 45% of the respondents also indicated their business is not profitable. Why do I mention this survey? Early in Section 1, I introduced a survey from McKinsey & Company that suggested why larger companies with multiple layers of management might be struggling in this current economic environment. In this discussion, I continue the same idea and discussion with smaller businesses (annual revenue between $1M and $200M) as the backdrop.

This discussion addresses the critical leadership functions of successfully setting goals and achieving desired results. In the survey above, not only were 45% of the surveyed companies not profitable; the same percentage of companies did not have specific, and measureable goals for their employees. The correlation is clear: having specific and measureable goals for employees impacts profitability.

So why do so few businesses have specific and measureable goals for their employees? I offer three reasons why this may be the case based on my own experience.

- ✓ **Lack of Vision for the Business** – Many small businesses make it up as they go by reacting to the ebb and flow of their specific industry and customer base. Without a clear direction, as the Cheshire Cat in Alice in Wonderland said, "any road will take you there." The view of what the business is doing is typically through the rear view mirror.

Section 3: Organizational Leadership

- ✓ **Ill-defined Strategy** – Strategy reflects the competitive direction of a business. How does the business compete in its industry? An ill-defined strategy creates a scenario where there is little substance to anchor organizational or individual goals to. Uncertainty of what is happening in the industry and with the competition makes it very difficult to establish SMART (Specific, Measureable, Attainable, Reasonably High and Time-Bound) goals for employees and align them to the business strategy.

- ✓ **Measuring Activities versus Results** – Even if a business has established goals tied to an overall strategy, if they can't measure progress, a negative outcome still results. It is important to ensure the business is tracking and measuring results, not activities, and doing so in a manner that yields new knowledge as opposed to restating or repackaging existing information.

How do your goals reflect your business strategy?

Lead Well!

Section 3: Organizational Leadership

Don't Love Your Business Idea...
Love the Problem You Want to Solve

Simon Sinek made a name for himself in his book "Start With Why" by codifying the Golden Circle. The Golden Circle is actually three concentric circles with the word "Why" in the center circle, the word "What" on the middle circle and the word "How" in the outer circle. He uses the diagram to explain the importance of starting with "Why" versus "How," as many businesses do today. I believe Eric Paley's quote above also speaks to the importance of looking at Success from the Client's point of view

In my experience, the tendency is to get too internally focused on the business idea, losing focus on the external problem the idea solves. I find this is especially true with leaders who've led their organizations for a long time. As we get into the conversation of what's going on in the organization, I will typically and offhandedly ask, "Tell me again, why you started/joined this business?" The answers are varied and indicate where they really are in the internal versus external mindset.

So how does a leader stay focused on the Problem to Solve? The key to successful focus is to be crystal clear on the "Why." Leaders who actively engage themselves and their organization in the Strategic Thinking process are never very far from the "Why" because it is an active part of their leadership credo. The Strategic Thinking process consists of creating a Vision Statement, a Mission Statement and Strategic Objectives to define how the organization will solve problems to effectively compete.

The Vision Statement provides the foundation for why an organization or business does what it does. It paints the picture of a future the organization or business aspires to. It also provides the leader a point of reference to keep the organization focused on the desired result (solve the problem) versus activity (business idea).

The Mission Statement provides the leader with the means to take the ideas embedded in the Vision Statement and articulate them in a very tangible way to the organization.

Section 3: Organizational Leadership

The Strategic Objectives determine how the organization or business is going to compete. When a business has a clear Vision of why it is in business and can clearly articulate what it will do to make the Vision a reality through its Mission, identifying the Strategy becomes surprisingly clear and straightforward. However, when leaders create a Strategy without the Vision and Mission, they are more often reacting to the market and are more enamored by their business ideas than the problems they are aiming to solve.

What problem does your organization love to solve today?

Lead Well!

Section 3: Organizational Leadership

You Cannot Control The Wind...
But You Can Adjust The Sails

These words to the Ricky Skaggs song *Can't Control The Wind* are a great entrée into a discussion of the Total Leadership Model (see Appendix A). These particular words came to mind as I was reading a Fortune article several years ago about Larry Ellison and the BMW Oracle Racing Team returning the America's Cup Trophy back to the United States after a fifteen-year absence. His thoughts on the victory centered on the right combination of technology, sailing skills and strategy.

Strategy forms the foundation of the Total Leadership Process and reflects the Purpose of the organization. In actuality, the organizational Purpose is a combination of Vision, Values, Mission and Strategy, but it is the Strategy that determines how the organization will compete in its current market and industry. Understanding the importance of this definition is crucial, as the competitive assumptions in every industry are changing.

What strategic assumptions worked when economic and industry growth rates were 10% - 15% before the most recent recession will be different in the 2% - 3% growth economy of the recovery. Likewise, targeting double-digit growth rates will require different strategic assumptions than in previous years where that level of growth was not the norm. A strategy setting a path to 12% growth year-over-year sounds good at face value. However, if the industry is growing 15%, the strategy loses market share.

Like the wind challenges sailors, we may have difficulty totally understanding and reacting to the competitive landscape. Some events we can see well in advance. For instance, the recent healthcare reform legislation was announced well in advance, enabling organizations to think through various contingency plans on how to react to the final version.

Section 3: Organizational Leadership

Other competitive events are not well known, yet must be anticipated in order to put forth a reasonable strategy for success. Most of us cannot accurately predict the future. But the issue is not to predict the future; it is to prepare for the future. Successful leaders continuously run scenarios for their market or industry helping them adapt quickly to their changing competitive landscape.

With so many changes happening at an ever-increasing rate, do you have a means to capture what your market is telling your organization every day in a way that is meaningful to the contingency scenarios relevant to your strategy? Ask yourself how much time your organization spends managing the past versus navigating towards the future. If we drove our cars the same way, how much progress would we make?

When the wind changes direction, which way will your crew be facing?

Lead Well!

Section 3: Organizational Leadership

If You Can't Describe What You Do as a Process…
You Don't Know What You Are Doing

These words from W. Edwards Deming, considered the godfather of organizational process improvement, are a great way to discuss the Operational Improvement component of the Total Leadership Model (see Appendix A). To put it in perspective, Strategy is the foundation of the model and Leadership Development is one of the two key supporting elements of the model. We now look at Operational Improvement, the Process side of Total Leadership, as the other supporting element crucial to being an effective leader in today's business environment.

Everything we do in our organization, be it public, private, non-profit, large or small is a process. Everything we do has inherent interdependencies between what happens before, during and after each task and function we execute. And because each task and function we execute has an outcome, it becomes a point in which we can measure the desired results. In Dr. H. James Harrington's book, *Business Process Improvement,* he puts it this way:

- ✔ "Measurements are key.

- ✔ If you cannot measure it, you cannot control it.

- ✔ If you cannot control it, you cannot manage it.

- ✔ If you cannot manage it, you cannot improve it.

- ✔ It is as simple as that."

Section 3: Organizational Leadership

At this point, there may be those of you who may be thinking, "This is great, but I don't operate in the plant or in operations where our products are made." In truth, more than half of the Operational Improvement opportunities are in the traditional "front office" functions such as Sales, Marketing, Finance and Human Resources. Or there may be those entrepreneurs who run small businesses who think this is great for larger companies but does not apply to small businesses. In fact, missing these opportunities for Operational Improvement likely has a much greater financial impact on small businesses as a percentage of revenue than in the larger companies. It's akin to thinking gravity does not apply to you because you weigh less than twenty pounds. All processes have very real financial impacts if not producing their desired results!

Today's leaders see this as an opportunity to truly understand what they do in the context of a global business environment that is constantly evolving through regulatory, economic and socio-cultural changes. As a leader, it's not enough to merely invest in people in the organization if you are not also willing to ensure the processes they use are optimized for success.

So, describe what you do again?

Lead Well!

Section 3: Organizational Leadership

We Need 100%...
From 100%

As a leader in corporate organizations, the military and small businesses, I used this as a frequent reminder to my organization that we all have a role to play in our organization's success. I also reminded them of the importance of showing up every day with everything they have to give, not just show up. Said differently, I was promoting full employee engagement by everyone in the organization. In the Total Leadership Model (see appendix A), it all centers on the level of engagement by employees, associates and volunteers who create the moments of truth, or points of connection, between the organization and those who bring you business.

Gallup Poll surveys consistently indicate that, in average performing organizations, only 33% of employees are engaged in the business. Compare this to world-class organizations where the exact opposite is true, 67% of the organization is engaged in the business. In addition, in average performing organizations, 18% of the employees were actively disengaged. This means that only a third of the organization cares about the activities contributing directly to employee retention, productivity, customer satisfaction/engagement, safety and profitability; all measurable dimensions of organizational success. Improving employee engagement has a direct effect on customer loyalty. Even a 5% increase in customer loyalty can improve profits by at least 25% and up to 85%, depending on industry.

But what if you are a small- or medium-sized business with few employees? Does this matter? How engaged are the employees of your larger customers, especially the ones who implement your services, purchase your products and pay your invoices? If they don't care beyond the minimum, how does that affect your business? Employee engagement impacts every business, large or small!

Section 3: Organizational Leadership

And engagement starts with leadership. Jack Welch, former CEO of General Electric, once said, "Any company trying to compete...must figure out how to engage the mind of every employee." We define organizational culture as the shared value, beliefs and actions that develop within an organization, guiding the behavior of its members. Employee attitude is where success originates for leaders because attitude drives behavior, and behavior drives the achievement of desired results for the organization. The behavior observed by your customers, suppliers and other employees forms the ongoing perception of your organization and your business.

As you understand the market's perception of your business, are you getting 100% out of 100%?

Lead Well!

Section 3: Organizational Leadership

Your Mission...
Should You Choose To Accept It

Many of you recognize this line from the television series or movie (or both, depending on your generation) Mission: Impossible. Several years ago, I had the privilege of delivering the Keynote Address to a group of military veterans at a career transition event the day after Veterans Day. The theme of Mission is one our military veterans clearly understand so the other speakers and I leveraged the same theme throughout the event.

We talk about information overload and its impact on a leader's ability to make knowledgeable decisions. I would submit having a clear sense of Mission is just as important as information in making meaningful decisions since it creates the tangible importance of making the decision in the first place. When a leader loses the understanding of importance, the overall mission begins to falter. We see organizations in many corners of our environment that have lost their sense of mission. In recent years, we have seen examples of government, financial, religious and educational institutions with documented lapses in their sense of mission.

So how do leaders renew their sense of Mission? They must first ask themselves, "Why do we exist?" Corporations, Entrepreneurial ventures and Not-For-Profits all exist for a defined purpose. The second question every organization must ask is, "Whom do we serve?" We use the word "serve" specifically because it creates a service mindset as opposed to asking, "To whom do we sell?" or "Who is in our market?" Whenever I work with clients whose business has hit a plateau, I always start with some variation of that same question. In answering the question of whom they serve, they start to renew their sense of Mission.

Section 3: Organizational Leadership

The sense of Mission also implies the entire organization is engaged to effectively complete it. Leaders must be able to effectively communicate the Mission to their teams. Herein lies part of the challenge – they may not know how to communicate or they overestimate their ability to do so. A survey by Developmental Dimensions International and published in the Wall Street Journal suggests managers struggle with the necessary skills necessary to execute a sense of organizational mission. Of 1,100 respondents, only 36% felt they were strong in coaching their teams while only 34% felt they were strong in gaining commitment from their teams. Lastly, only 32% mentioned delegating as their strength. These types of blind spots can cause an organization's leaders to lose their way.

Great leaders have a sense of Mission as well as personal accountability to that Mission and those they serve.

As you canvas your competitive landscape, what Mission will you choose to accept?

Lead Well!

Section 3: Organizational Leadership

Are You Playing to Win or...
Playing Not to Lose?

In today's challenging business environment, the answer to this question can make or break the ability to achieve sustainable success. I can recall many a sports team that led most of an important game with a strategy to win. With a comfortable lead going into the final period, the team shifted to a strategy of playing "not to lose" (either mentally, physically or both) and lost. Business leaders must also be aware of engaging to win or merely not to lose. Let's take a quick look at the difference and how these strategies impact the organization's long-term success.

Playing Not to Lose (Reactive):

- **Negating Problems** – Organizations playing not to lose typically focus on negating problems. Taken to an extreme, these organizations end up playing a big game of whack-a-mole where the problems are the pop-up characters in the game.

- **Cutting Expenses to Enhance Profit** – While reducing expenses is necessary from time to time, organizations using this strategy as a regular lift to enhance quarterly profit margins are playing not to lose.

- **Bashing the Competition to Win** – My grandmother used to say, "Don't make your candle shine brighter by blowing the other person's candle out." In a competitive process, if an organization only speaks to bash the competition, they are ultimately playing not to lose.

Section 3: Organizational Leadership

Playing to Win (Proactive):

- ✓ **Creating Opportunities –** Organizations that create opportunities for themselves, even in tough economic times, are playing to win. In many cases, these organizations end up re-writing the rules of the game itself in their industry or market as they create their new opportunities.

- ✓ **Growing Revenue –** Organizations that play to win recognize you cannot cut your way to long term profitability and effectively leverage the existing organization to increase revenue. They are generally adept at deciding what they will not sell anymore as much as what else they will sell.

- ✓ **Selling their Value above all else –** A common phrase I come across is the Unique Value Proposition. Organizations that are crystal clear on their value proposition can leverage it with passion and rarely have to worry about discussing the competition, let alone bash them to be competitive.

Organizational Strategic Plans rarely consciously state whether they are playing not to lose or playing to win. However, their strategies usually tell the tale in the way organization's leaders execute them.

What is your game plan to Win?

Lead Well!

Section 3: Organizational Leadership

Change Occurs…
At The Outer Edge of Your Comfort Zone

At times in our leadership careers, many of us reflect on what we accomplished in the current business cycle and what changes we will make to continue our successes into the next. In my own work with small and medium for-profit and non-profit businesses, managing change is the most common topic of conversation and why not? The current economic and political environments have leaders in the unenviable position of making the next right strategic decision in the face of persistent uncertainty.

How do leaders mitigate this uncertainty enough to make the crucial decisions before them? While there are many moving parts to a successful business strategy, two elements of leading any organization are: understanding your general competitive environment and knowing how your current capabilities match up to that environment. Any leader's key strategic thinking process includes a recurring assessment of their environment against six different factors: Economic, Global, Demographic/Psychographic, Political/Legal, Socio-Cultural and Technical. All six factors will influence your ability to adapt and evolve your business. Ask yourself how they impact your business, non-profit or corporation.

- ✓ **Economic** – While the recession may be over, businesses are generally still taking a cautious road ahead which has a direct impact on the economic recovery.

- ✓ **Global** – You may not be a global business, but events around the globe impact your business. Have you figured out how and why?

- ✓ **Demographic/Psychographic** – We are seeing the impact of the latest census and changing U.S. demographics. Psychographics reflect the personalities, values and attitudes of the population.

- ✓ **Political/Legal** – All eyes are on Washington, D.C. these days to gauge the impact of Congress' decisions on the current level of cautiousness across the business landscape.

Section 3: Organizational Leadership

- ✓ **Socio-Cultural** – We see more and more organizations hiring temporary workers, including management and other predominantly white-collar positions.

- ✓ **Technical** – An article in the 12/20/10 Wall Street Journal opines how Dr. Seuss would love the e-Readers because they enable children to read more effectively. Is technology effectively advancing your business?

We know change is inevitable, but business growth due to change is not. I am reminded of the closing scene in The Truman Show when Jim Carrey's Truman finally makes it to the outer edge of his known world. After a brief dialog, Truman opens the door, literally and figuratively, to a whole new world of possibilities.

When you get to the outer edge of your comfort zone, how are you prepared to open the door to new possibilities?

Lead Well!

Section 3: Organizational Leadership

Effectively balancing the "What"...
versus the "How" as a Leader

One of the most challenging balancing acts a leader faces is determining how much to communicate what they want the desired results and outcomes to be versus how much they instruct those who execute the business on how to achieve the desired results and outcomes. I would imagine your first response might be something along the lines of, "Whatever it takes to achieve the goals," or, possibly, "If you want it done right, you need to tell them exactly how to do it." However, if you view the role of leader against the long-term view of business success, the answer is not so simple.

One would think communicating what to do would be the easier of the two tasks. I maintain they are both equally challenging for completely different reasons. It starts with translating the Vision of the business into a meaningful and tangible language for those who execute the business goals. Because the leader cannot possibly communicate every minute detail of the strategy, they must outline enough of the "What" and "Why" for the strategy to succeed. In other words, leaders must communicate their intent to the organization, which can be a big challenge.

Every leader must ask themselves, "What does Success look like?" and clearly communicate the answer. When the business is successful, what are people in the business doing? What are customers of the business saying about you? What are your vendors doing to support you? The more detailed the answers, the clearer the leader's intent. Notice there is no mention of how all this occurs, only that when success does occur, this is the picture we see.

Section 3: Organizational Leadership

Which brings us to communicating how to achieve the desired results. The process begins with an accurate assessment of the Attitudes, Skills and Knowledge of the team. We know that Attitude, or the Want to Succeed, is 75% of the overall success equation. If those who execute the business do not believe they can carry out the strategy the leader communicates to them, it is a foregone conclusion it will fail. If they believe in the strategy, success is three quarters complete! The team must also possess the requisite Skills, or how to do the functions to succeed, and the Knowledge, knowing when and where to leverage the requisite skills for overall success.

Understanding the necessary Attitudes, Skills and Knowledge in the context of the leader's intent presents its own challenge because leaders may have differing perspectives than those who execute the business. As Anais Nin once said, "We don't see things as they are; we see them as we are." It all starts with effectively communicating a strategy and strategic intent to those who execute the business.

If a total stranger walks up to you and asks you to describe what your success looks like, how clear is the picture you paint for them?

Lead Well!

Section 3: Organizational Leadership

"You treat a disease, you win or you lose. ...
You treat a person, I guarantee you, you'll win,
no matter what the outcome"

This quote from Dr. Hunter "Patch" Adams coincides with a recent video blog by Dr. Mark Hyman addressing how the evolution of healthcare means changing our thinking from "the drug for the bug and the pill for the ill" to viewing the human body as an eco-system. While systems thinking is not a new concept, when it is applied to the healthcare field that traditionally looks to fix the part without looking at the whole system, it does take on new meaning. 21st Century leaders, regardless of their organizational scope or circumstance, face similar challenges. The best leaders can see these challenges holistically rather than single short-term issues to solve. So how do leaders improve their systems thinking ability?

By quick review, systems thinking means understanding how a single element under investigation interacts with other elements in the system. The idea breaks down into five key elements of a simple system: Source, Input, Process, Output and Target.

A Source provides some form of Input to the Process, which manipulates the Input to produce an Output intended for a specific Target. While simply stated, successful leaders understand the impact the whole system has on the part and just as important, how the solution (output) will now impact the whole system.

By way of example, I was once faced with a difficult customer situation where we knew we would not be able to deliver 100% on the customer's request because we fully understood the issue from a systems point of view. We committed to 65% while other competitors committed to 100%. At the end of the day, our company and competitors all landed in the 67% range because the whole system impacted everyone in the same way. Our understanding of the system allowed us to operate in the right context and create a loyal customer!

Section 3: Organizational Leadership

One of the best tools for understanding the system comes from the world of process improvement: the Five Whys. The concept begins with asking why a problem or issue has occurred. The answer then generates another question around why that situation exists and on and on until the questioning is at last five layers deep. While used for root cause analysis, I find the five whys provide a broader view of the key inputs and outputs as the questions are asked and answered.

As Dr. Patch Adams and Dr. Mark Hyman viewed the whole person as the subject of medical treatment, so successful leaders view the whole system in the context of their decisions. Because every system has a unique set of boundaries, systems thinking can easily apply to any leader regardless of their scope of responsibility.

How are you defining the whole system that supports your business?

Lead Well!

Section 3: Organizational Leadership

"Lather, Rinse, Repeat"

Look on any bottle of shampoo and you will see some variation of these three words. The concept of repetition is at the heart of successful and sustainable leadership development. Leadership development must be a continuous process for every leader in every organization regardless of circumstances. Organizations of all size benefit from investment in leadership development and the effective use of repetition to embed the new attitudes and behaviors that contribute to achieving desired results.

An oft-quoted expression goes, "Change is inevitable, Growth is not!" Change is the first reason why repetition must be integral to leadership development. Practice makes us good at things (sports, music, etc.) was because repetition yields proficiency. In business, the environment around us is always changing, creating a need to change to stay relevant. Practice these repetitive habits to keep up with change:

- When faced with scenarios challenging the status quo, begin your questioning with a form of "What if...?" or "Why not...?"

- Re-validate the environment every six months to ensure your business assumptions are still relevant to your business strategy.

The second reason for repetitive leadership development is Effective Communications. In a global economy with four generations in the workforce, a leader's ability to communicate effectively may well be the difference between success and failure. Practice these repetitive habits to communicate more effectively:

- Communicate the meaning of the message, especially around mission critical content.

- Become adept at asking effective open-ended questions to draw out the true level of understanding and help the leader become a more effective listener.

Section 3: Organizational Leadership

The final reason to use repetition in leadership development is Goal Achievement. Leaders set goals and achieve desired results. These goals will succeed far greater than those that are vague, unwritten and do not align to the organization's Strategy. Practice these repetitive habits to achieve goals more effectively:

- ✔ Until goals are written down and communicated, they are not really goals.

- ✔ Use affirmations to support your positive mindset. When a positive attitude meets obstacles, the attitude will prevail!

How are you using repetition to develop your leadership skills? How are you using repetition to develop your leadership skills?

Lead Well!

Section 3: Organizational Leadership

Hope is Not a Strategy!

We cannot hope for success! Yet how many times a day do we say so without even realizing it? In what has become one of my all time favorite quotes, this title of Rick Page's book is a constant reminder to me that whatever we successfully do as leaders, we must do with a defined purpose that leverages all of our available resources to achieve our goals. In the nearly 20 years of applying this idea to a plethora of businesses, I have come to realize how important business alignment is to achieving sustainable success.

In *The Missing Piece: Creating Sustainable Success Through Business Alignment,* I define business alignment as "the process of matching the organization's tactics to the available or readily acquirable resources to achieve its strategic objectives." The real question is, "How do we do that in our business, especially in today's challenging business environment?" The first step is to understand the three main elements of business alignment: Strategic Thinking, Operational Support Elements and Tactical Execution.

The Strategic Thinking process helps define the general direction of the organization. In this context, it consists of creating the organization's Vision of a desired future, a Mission Statement to create a tangible direction for the organization and a Strategy specifically defining how the organization will compete in its markets and industry.

The Operational Support Elements are the "available or readily available resources" necessary to achieve the strategic objectives. They consist of the right People, Processes, Technology and Rewards Systems the organization has in place to successfully execute the tactics. Emphasis on the right resources is crucial because organizations likely have resources that might have been right in the past but may or may not be the right People, Processes, Technology and Rewards for the future strategy of the organization.

Section 3: Organizational Leadership

Tactical Execution consists of the Goals and Scientific Methodologies needed to achieve the Desired Results for the organization. The Goals must align throughout the organization lest they run at cross-purposes with one another. The Scientific Methods determine how to track and measure the goals to ensure the goals are achieving not just any results but the desired results the organization needs to achieve its Strategy.

Regardless of the size or industry of the organization, the business alignment process has never turned less than double-digit growth when utilized to it fullest capability!

What does double-digit growth do for your business?

Lead Well!

Section 3: Organizational Leadership

Leadership Lessons from...
the Stanley Cup Champion Chicago Blackhawks!

The exciting finish to the 2013 Stanley Cup finals will stay fresh in our minds for quite some time (at least here in the Windy City!). Thinking about this victory presents an opportunity to look into leadership ideas from a championship journey in professional sports. In this case, the idea of teamwork and organizational alignment seem to be the very essence of the 2013 Chicago Blackhawks' success!

The story really begins in 2010 when the Blackhawks won the Stanley Cup against Philadelphia. Shortly after that game, the realities of free agency and the business side of professional sports forced the team to part ways with some of the outstanding players from that championship team. The realities of business are no different. Leaders will have to ask, "What is the right team to achieve future desired results?" It will not necessarily be the team that won the last championship or achieved past successes. Rather, it will need to be the team that will win the next championship and achieve the desired results of a constantly changing future business environment.

I can say from personal experience this level of leadership is not easy. Parting with popular players put Blackhawks management at odds with their customers, the fans. However, they forged ahead maintaining the nucleus of talent around which to build the next championship team. Business leaders face the same scrutiny. When I needed to downsize my organization after the 2001 Internet meltdown, I was faced with choices of cutting larger salaries that would cripple future growth or cutting more people and retaining a core group with which to build future business. I chose the latter, unpopular path. Always build for the next championship team!

Section 3: Organizational Leadership

"Teamwork" was probably the most used word in the media and post-game interviews regarding the team. Sometimes we hear professional athletes use the word and can tell they are coached to say it. In the Blackhawks case, you believed it was sincere and a true measure of their success. You would also need to include the front and back office personnel, who, I was glad to see, were mentioned in the media as well. Successful business leaders also understand success is not just on the shoulders of the few visible players. Sustainable success occurs when everyone is aligned around the Vision and Strategy and you get "100% from 100%" of the team.

Clearly, business is not governed by the rules of sports free agency in the strictest sense. However, like professional sports, the dynamics of the business will change from cycle to cycle and faster with time.

As you assess your current team, who will take you to your next championship, and what are you doing about the ones who won't?

Lead Well!

Appendix A

The Total Leadership Model

The Total Leadership Model provides an overall view of how Leadership creates the desired results of the business and/or organization. It serves as the backdrop for the leadership journey that begins with Purpose and moves through People and Process to create Moments of Truth that drive Profit.

Loyal Customers

Customers drive revenue; Loyal Customers drive PROFITABILITY. Therefore the goal of any organizational Strategy must be to create loyal customers to effectively compete in today's business environment.

Employees

It is through the alignment of People Management and Operational Systems to your Business Strategy that your organization's employees will maximize their Moments of Truth with your Customers and Create the Loyalty required for long term Profitability.

Operational Efficiency

Operational Efficiency addresses the way work will flow through your organization and the way it is structured to enable the Strategy to succeed. It is a reflection of how well the organization's operational PROCESSES are aligned.

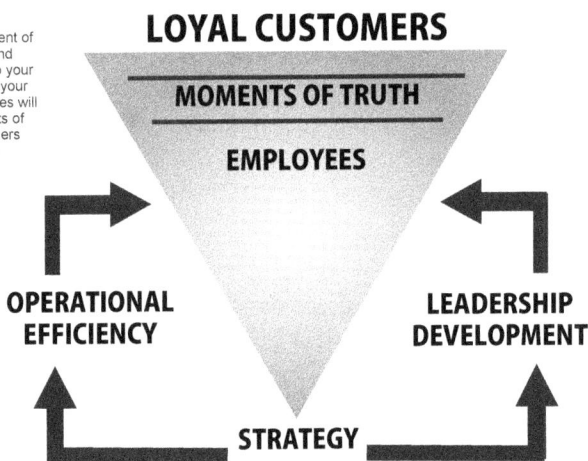

Strategy

Your Strategy speaks to how you will execute against your competition or our personal barriers during this business cycle (typically this current year). It is a reflection of your organization's PURPOSE as a business.

Leadership Development

Leadership Development addresses the way the organization is led by its leaders, managers and supervisors through communication, delegation and recognition of your organization's employees to enable the Strategy to succeed. It is a reflection of the organization's commitment to its PEOPLE.

Appendix B

Results!

The Business Alignment Maturity Model ©

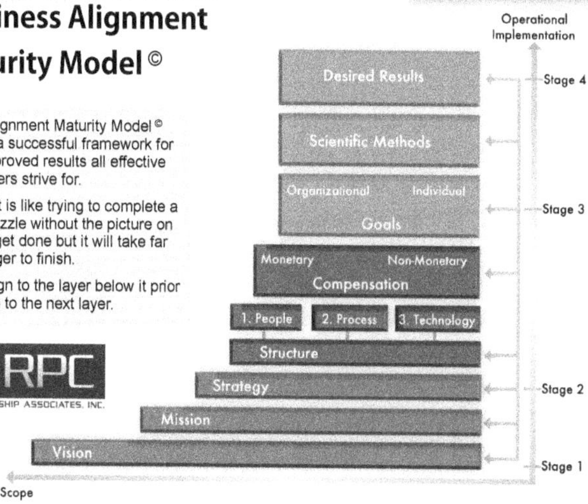
Operational Implementation
Desired Results
Scientific Methods
Organizational
Individual
Goals
Monetary
Non-Monetary
Compensation
1. People
2. Process
3. Technology
Structure
Strategy
Mission
Vision
Stage 4
Stage 3
Stage 2
Stage 1
Scope

The Business Alignment Maturity Model © [BAMM] provides a successful framework for achieving the improved results all effective leaders strive for.

Operating without it is like trying to complete a thousand piece puzzle without the picture on the box. It might get done but it will take far longer to finish.

Each layer must align to the layer below it prior to moving to the next layer.

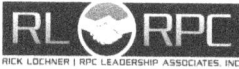

RL RPC
RICK LOCHNER | RPC LEADERSHIP ASSOCIATES, INC.

The Business Alignment Maturity Model ©

Vision – Your Vision outlines the organizational or personal direction for the future. Think of it as your "North Star" for the next 5 years.

Mission – Your Mission Statement adds more specificity to how you will accomplish your Vision over the next 2 to 3 years.

Strategy – Your Strategy speaks to how you will execute against your competition or your personal barriers during this business cycle (typically this current year).

Structure – Most organizations are organized vertically around processes that work horizontally. Structural alignment occurs when People, Processes and Technology work with the Strategy, not at cross-purposes with it.

1. **People:** *Organizations must continuously assess whether their people are capable and compatible with the Strategy, especially as it evolves.*
2. **Process:** *It is said that bad processes can ruin good people. Organizations must align their processes with the right people not the other way around.*
3. **Technology:** *Technology supports people and process. Organizations must ensure their technology is supporting, not inhibiting the Strategy.*

Compensation – Since Success comes from a positive change in Behaviors and Habits, how will you incent the right behaviors for your organization and/or yourself?

Goals – These are specific and detailed objectives required to successfully execute the Strategy. They are accompanied by Action Steps to outline in detail Who does What by When.

Scientific Methods – Along with Who, What and When you also need to determine How you will measure your progress toward your Strategy.

Results – The culmination of your planning and execution! The Business Alignment Model helps you articulate the Results in the context of your Strategy and ultimately your overall Vision.

RickLochner.com RL RPC RICK LOCHNER | RPC LEADERSHIP ASSOCIATES, INC. RickLochner.com

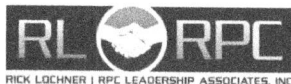

About the Author

Rick Lochner is the President and CEO of RPC Leadership Associates, Inc. He is an accomplished Coach, Facilitator, College Professor, Keynote and Workshop Speaker, Author and foremost, a Leader.

His Vision is to help Business Owners, Corporate and Non-Profit Leadership Teams and Individual Professionals Make Leadership a Way of Life. He coaches organizational leaders to leverage effective goal-setting, organizational planning, people development and process improvement to ensure their business strategies achieve their desired results.

Rick is a graduate of the United States Military Academy at West Point and spent his 11-year military career leading soldiers in challenging environments around the globe. After leaving the Army, he spent the next 18 years in corporate leadership positions ranging from front-line management to senior executive management. He successfully led organizations in Fortune 100 corporations and privately held entrepreneurial ventures across multiple industries.

In addition to his undergraduate studies Rick holds both an MS and MBA. He is a Visiting Professor at the Keller Graduate School of Management where he teaches a variety of leadership-related topics including 21st Century Leadership, Managing Organizational Conflict and Strategic Management.

Rick gives back to the local community as a member of the Board of Directors for Literacy DuPage as well as leading the nationally recognized Leadership Institute of the Naperville Area Chamber of Commerce. He and his wife Colleen reside in Naperville, IL.

Thank You!